The Reasonableness of Christianity
by Jonathan Dickinson
with chapters by C. Matthew McMahon

Copyright Information

The Reasonableness of Christianity, by Jonathan Dickinson with chapters by C. Matthew McMahon
Edited by Therese B. McMahon and Susan Ruth

Copyright ©2022 by Puritan Publications and A Puritan's Mind

Some language and grammar have been updated from the original manuscript. Any change in wording or punctuation has not changed the intent or meaning of the original authors, and has been made to aid the modern reader.

Published by Puritan Publications
A Ministry of A Puritan's Mind™ in Crossville, TN.
www.apuritansmind.com
www.puritanpublications.com

All rights reserved. No part of this publication may be reproduced, stored in a retrieval system or transmitted in any form by any means, electronic, mechanical, photocopy, recording or otherwise, without the prior permission of the publisher, except as provided by USA copyright law.

This Print Edition, 2022
Electronic Edition, 2022
Manufactured in the United States of America

eISBN: 978-1-62663-426-8
ISBN: 978-1-62663-427-5

Table of Contents

Fundamentals to Faith 4

Meet Jonathan Dickinson 11

To the Christian Reader 13

A Demonstration of the Being and Attributes of God 19

A Demonstration of the Apostate State of Man by Nature, and of the Glorious Provision Made for His Recovery by Jesus Christ 41

A Demonstration of the Christian Religion from the Prophesies of the Old Testament 69

A Demonstration of the Christian Religion from the Miracles Performed by our Lord Jesus Christ, both Before and After His Crucifixion 94

Other New and Helpful Works from Puritan Publications 133

Fundamentals to Faith
by C. Matthew McMahon, Ph.D., Th.D.

It is interesting to note that the catechisms of the *Westminster Confession* (and subsequently most other catechisms that were penned by the reformers) followed a line of thinking that covered three important areas of the Christian faith: 1) Basic theology, 2) The Ten Commandments, and 3) The Lord's Prayer. Both the Larger and Shorter catechisms were created specifically to teach the church the *fundamentals* of the Christian *faith*. In the *Shorter Catechism*, it was used to teach those of a "weaker capacity" to understand the *fundamental truths* of Scripture. These fundamentals are those aspects of the Christian faith which all believers should: 1) have an interest in, and, 2) understand to have a basic foundation of the Bible's truth. The *Shorter Catechism* was used to specifically teach *younger* children.[1] The Larger Catechism was used to teach people of age. Both Catechisms in their day were extensively helpful to aid the church in setting down basic Christian doctrine so that the best Reformed Churches were on the same page as to the teaching of the Bible. Today, this has been almost completely lost, and people are woefully ignorant of the basics of the Christian religion and of its fundamentals.

---

[1] Sadly, most older Christians today have no idea what the *Catechism* even says, much less, what it is.

If a professing Christian is ignorant of fundamental Christian truth, their capacity for reasoning becomes impaired. In the scope of God's redemptive plan and the manner in which he considers his chosen people as his church, his people and their children are of great importance as they relate to what they *know to be true* in his word. They are required by God to know the basic fundamentals of the faith, (in fact, they are required to know all the word of God). In *learning* such fundamentals, God says, "it is not a vain thing for you; because it is your life," (Deut. 32:47). And God's "case" against his people, his court-case that he often brings against his wayward people, frequently revolves around their failure to grasp and live out the basics of the Christians faith (the fundamentals of a rational and practical belief system), which in turn, brings in God's wrath and displeasure upon a people who reject his word by being disinterested in learning it. "My people are destroyed for lack of knowledge: because thou hast rejected knowledge, I will also reject thee," (Hosea 4:6). Scripture directs us that if we train up our children in the way they should go, when they are old they will not depart from those teachings. This is not an easy task, but, it is a commanded one. God says, "Train up a child in the way he should go: and when he is old, he will not depart from it," (Proverbs 22:6). That seems important! What will you teach them?

With such a daunting responsibility as to be good stewards of holy covenant children, as well as of our own faithfulness in the study and exploration of God's truth, it is the Christian's responsibility (not the local Sunday school class) to teach our families how to be good Christians. This requires we learn the fundamentals, have the ability to think through those fundamentals, and why theological history has been so enamored with teaching those basics throughout its entire history. Parenting does not only include physical correction and training to obey parents (such as eating all their dinner that is placed in front of them), but more specifically spiritual correction and discipline. God says, "Gather me the people together, and I will make them hear my words, that they may learn to fear me all the days that they shall live upon the earth, and that they may *teach their children*," (Deut. 4:10). Jesus was especially concerned with covenant children and their well-being when he said, "Suffer the little children to come unto me, and forbid them not: for of such is the kingdom of God," (Mark 10:14). This verse, and Matthew 19:14 which quote Mark 10:14, uses the term "such a one" to refer to children. If God and Christ hold such a high regard for children since they are the future theologians and ministers of the church, so should we. We should care not only for our *own* spiritual well-being, but also of all those in our own families and in the household of faith.

    Today's church is woefully ignorant of the basics of the Christian religion. People often think that if they know Jesus loves them, and this they know because the bible tells them so, they have enough to get to heaven regardless of what other doctrines and biblical teaching they may be ignorant of. What they tend to replace the bible with is that song, "Jesus loves me." Sadly, this is as much as they *want* to know about what *the bible tells them*. But how does Jesus love them? What does he do to love them? Who is he to love them? Why does he love them? What does he require of those he loves? *etc*. Whole scores of "reformed ministers" and "reformed laymen" just want to make sure the people in their church know that "Jesus loves them" and that such sentiments are "enough." Folks of that "happy clappy" watered-down contemporary flavor are going to find Jonathan Dickinson too heady and difficult to even give a listen.

Dickinson's work before you is one of *fundamentals*. He has chosen four areas of the fundamentals of the faith (basic Christian theology) to bring to you its *reasonableness*. It is both a Scriptural and rational endeavor to understand the basics of the Christian faith and jettison you into the larger branches of basic Christian truth. Certainly, these branches can be found in the catechisms of the church, but in this succinct form (in only 4 sermons), they are a grand help to the learning Christian. Learning Christians, those *running* down the highway of holiness, want both to know what God says about himself and what God requires of them in their life of the pursuit of holiness. Sadly, his sermons may seem over cerebral for most Christians, but that is because Christians today do not *like to think* about fundamentals, rather, they are content to accept only the most basic idea that any person who has ever heard of Jesus may comply with. "Oh, yes, I know that I am going to heaven because Jesus loves me ... that little diddy of a song tells me so." And it is there that they leave their theology to their own detriment. Dickinson is going to make Christians *think*, and while thinking, show them the nature of fundamental Christianity, *i.e.* that it is reasonable (because God is reasonable) and it directly distills truth about the perfections and character of the most high God (which is the very reason Jesus came, John 1:18, to *declare* the Father). Not only does it encapsulate the fundamentals of the faith, but it is *rational*. The Christian Gospel is rational and can be shown to be rational. Why? Again, *God* is rational. The Christian faith, therefore, does not contain an ounce of blind faith. When church-going people tell you that they "just believe" the Bible without any proof for believing, they are being *moronic*. Is that too harsh? It is God's case against them who speak that way, "The fear of the LORD is the beginning of knowledge: but *fools* despise wisdom and instruction," (Prov. 1:7). Is *God* too harsh?

Christianity is not set upon blind faith – *ever*. God never requires anything irrational of his rational creatures. To believe something without evidence would be irrational. He does not require faith without knowledge, or faith in the impossible, or faith without evidence. The fundamentals of the Christian religion fuel our faith, without which we have just some form of knowledge – and the *devil* has that. The Bible gives ample evidence for all it teaches, and faith rests on what is known and contained in the Bible to be true about the God who *has* spoken. Are you aware of what he has rationally spoken about in the propositions of his word? Or are you among the myriads of Christian professors who have yet to read the bible one time through?

Dickinson, in this cause of showing forth the rational and reasonable aspects of the fundamentals of the faith will cover, in four sermons, the being and attributes of God, the rational evidence of man's fall in the garden, the mediation of the man Christ Jesus, the evidence of Christ's work and merit from Old Testament prophecy, and the New Testament argument from miracles performed by Jesus Christ. Or, as Foxcroft says in the introductory chapter, Dickinson links together, "a numerous train of arguments drawn together in a comprehensive manner that deserve very attentive consideration." With such attentive consideration, by the end of the work, you will come away with the fundamentals of the faith, and the reasonableness of the Christian religion. This will, in turn, help you impart the truth of the basics of Christianity to the people in your family, and in your church. It will help you to grow, and them to grow, into a more vital union with Jesus Christ as you traverse the highway of holiness, without which, one will not see the Lord (Heb. 12:14).

In his abundant grace,
C. Matthew McMahon, Th.D., Ph.D.
From my study, January, 2022
"...search the Scriptures..." (John 5:39).

Meet Jonathan Dickinson
Edited by C. Matthew McMahon, Ph.D., Th.D.

Jonathan Dickinson, (1688–1747), was an American Presbyterian minister of the Gospel, and founder and first president of the College of New Jersey. He was born in Hatfield, MA., and graduated Yale in 1706. *The Great Awakening* that started in the 1730s profoundly changed religion in the American colonies. During this time, the Presbyterians were divided into, "New Sides," and, "Old Sides," supporters and opponents, respectively, of the great revival meetings and the fervent preaching that accompanied them. Dickinson was a *moderate new sider*, supporting the revivals while opposing their more violent excess. His pulpit oratory was centered on, "temperance and harmony," and, "devoid of antagonizing divisions, but which at the same time was appealing and innovative."[2] Dickinson was a strong supporter of Presbyterianism

---

[2] Choiński, Michal. *Rhetoric of the Revival: The Language of the Great Awakening Preachers.* (Vandenhoeck & Ruprecht, 2016). p. 166.

and earned a reputation as a leading defender of Calvinism in America.

Convinced of the need of an educational institution to carry forward the ideals of William Tennent (1673-1746), he obtained a charter (in 1746) for the College of New Jersey (now Princeton University). In 1747, he opened the institution at his house in Elizabethtown (now Elizabeth), N.J.[3]

---

[3] *The Columbia Electronic Encyclopedia*, 6th ed.

To the Christian Reader

The reverend and learned author of the ensuing discourses does not need any letters of commendation to those who are acquainted with his person and character. His praise is in the Gospel throughout all the churches in those remote areas where divine providence has taken him. Neither is he unknown to the public, which has been favored with several lesser writings of his, formerly published on special occasions. These writings must have left a positive impression on the minds of those who read them, and such an idea of Mr. Dickinson's peculiar genius, capacity, and judgment prepares them to come with raised expectations and a particular enthusiasm to the following work. It would be thought vain of me to attempt a profuse and glowing praise of them, for the known modesty of the author would prefer I not take this liberty.

And yet I must say that in reading these pages I have thought myself very agreeably entertained with the variety and expanse of thought, excellency of matter, strength of argument, and liveliness of expression. And I also believe that every serious discerning reader will find the beams of divine light shining round this revelation of the Gospel that has been exposed here with such force as cannot fail to give power and energy to faith and love, establish one in the principles and duties of Christianity, and guard him against the attacks of infidelity on all sides.

To the Christian Reader

The general design of this work is suggested in the title;[4] yet it may be appropriate to open the way to reading these sermons by first giving a summary of the whole work.

The first sermon is on the being and attributes of God, where we are led into deep and entertaining contemplations of his divine nature by a particular view of the eminent perfections of God as illustrated in the works of creation.

The second sermon gives us the rational evidence of our apostacy from God, and then carries us into a delightful meditation on our recovery by a Mediator. Its unparalleled intrinsic excellencies are considered. Its perfect congruity to all the divine prerogatives and illustration of the attributes of God, its correspondence to the nature and necessities of man, and conduciveness to our present welfare and future everlasting happiness are all set in view. A numerous train of arguments are

---

[4] *The Reasonableness of Christianity, in four sermons. Wherein the being and attributes of God, the apostasy of man, and the credibility of the Christian religion, are demonstrated by rational considerations. And the divine mission of our blessed Savior proved by Scripture-arguments, both from the Old Testament and the New; and vindicated against the most important objections, whether of ancient or modern infidels.* By Jonathan Dickinson, M.A. Minister of the Gospel at Elisabeth-Town, New Jersey. *Cum dilectione fides Christiani: Sine dilectione fides daemonum: Qui autem non credunt, pejores sunt quam daemones.* —Augustine, de Charit. With a Preface by Mr. Foxcroft. (BOSTON, New England: Printed by S. Kneeland, 1732).

drawn together in a comprehensive manner that deserve very attentive consideration.

The other discourses point out to us the one Mediator between God and men, the man Christ Jesus; and by many infallible proofs demonstrate that he is the true Messiah.

The third sermon considers the evidence from prophecy. It explains the nature of a prophecy as it is to be understood in the present argument and sets forth the various ways in which divine predictions may be said to be fulfilled. He instances some of the more signal prophecies of the Old Testament relating to the Messiah, his person and character, the time, circumstances, and consequences of his appearing. He then shows from the evangelical historians that they have been literally and exactly verified in Jesus of Nazareth. And finally, to complete the demonstration, it is shown that the united accomplishment of them all in the blessed Jesus is a loud testimony from heaven that he is the predicted Savior and justifies his claim to the high titles, perfections, and relations attributed to the Messiah in the prophetic descriptions of his person and kingdom.

The fourth and last sermon is upon the argument from miracles, where we have the correct notion of a miracle briefly stated. He shows that there were true and proper miracles performed by our Lord Jesus Christ, in his own person and by his apostles in his name. Then it is shown how those miraculous operations illustrate the truth of his divine mission and the certainty of his being the promised Messiah. These infer that the New Testament is that admirable collection of divine revelations written by inspired penmen, preserved, and transmitted in authentic copies, without any material depravation, down to the present age.

Finally, the author having demonstrated the divine authority and reasonableness of the Christian institution, concludes with some wise and good rules to settle the minds of wavering professors and direct persons convinced of the truth of Christianity in general how they may resolve their doubts, fix their choice, and determine in what way, mode, or form they may best serve Christ, to his acceptance and their own eternal advantage.

I have now given the reader a short and imperfect table of contents; a view of the principal scope and tenor of the discourses here exhibited to the public light. They are surely upon the noblest subjects, sublime in their nature, useful in their tendency, and seasonable for this skeptical day; and a particular application of them are useful for practice and devotion, which runs through and enlivens the work which is adapted to impress and engage the heart as well as employ the mind, to warm the Christian as well as please and improve the scholar.

In perusing this little volume, I do not doubt you'll be ready to break out in the language of the apostle: "this is a faithful saying, and worthy of all acceptation, that Christ Jesus came into the world to save sinners." And "without controversy great is the mystery of godliness. God was manifest in the flesh, justified in the Spirit, seen of angels, preached unto the Gentiles, believed on in the world, received up into glory." And "God forbid, that I should glory, save in the cross of our Lord Jesus Christ."

You will find that the only wise God our Savior has taken all possible care for our satisfaction in the certainty of revealed religion, and he does not challenge our belief of the Gospel without giving us sufficient grounds to examine the credentials it brings with it.

I am sure you will see all the marks of divinity evident on the Christian institution and know you will be ready to say with the apostle, "I am not ashamed of the Gospel of Christ, though I suffer reproach as a Christian, nevertheless I am not ashamed; for I know whom I have believed." You will see the apostle had good grounds for that exhortation, "be not ashamed of the testimony of our Lord, nor of me his prisoner."

It is fit and reasonable that we should submit to credible testimony; and if we receive the witness of men, the witness of God is greater. He therefore that does not believe God, in the record that he gave of his Son, makes himself to be a liar. No man rejects the principles of Christianity because his reason runs counter to them, but because his lusts control his reason and corrupt his judgment.

I will hasten therefore to a close with the statement that our first desire should be that the spirit of Christ may cause the light of the glorious Gospel to shine into our hearts and testify to its truth and divine origin by making it instrumental to an indelible impression of the image of Christ on our souls. And let it be our next and constant concern that by visibly exhibiting this inward experience in an active life of universal conformity to the example and laws of Christ, we may give a solid attestation to the reality of our faith and adorn the doctrine of God our Savior as it becomes us in all things. In this way evidencing ourselves sincere followers, living witnesses for Christ, that we may hope for his approval in this world and a glorious reception in the next.

To promote and spread the genuine spirit and practice of Christianity is the ultimate design of the following essay. And to that happy end may the special blessing of Christ accompany all those into whose hands it may come!

These are the unfeigned sentiments and passionate wishes of,

Your Christian friend,
Thomas Foxcroft.
Boston, February 29, 1731.

A Demonstration of the Being and Attributes of God

Romans 1:20, "For the invisible things of Him, from the creation of the world, are clearly seen, being understood by the things that are made, even his eternal power and Godhead; so that they are without excuse."

Reason is the dignifying and distinguishing property of human nature by which man, above the rest of the lower creation, is qualified to know, obey, and enjoy his Creator. By which he is capable of that faith; and without which it is *impossible* to please God. We believe that *God is*, as well as that he is a rewarder of those that diligently seek him. It follows that he who has made us rational creatures expects from us a *reasonable* service and cannot be pleased with that faith, practice, or hope that is grounded on education or common opinion instead of the result of rational reflection or inquiry.

It must therefore be agreeable both to our duty and interest to inquire into the grounds of our holy religion and to establish ourselves in those precious truths on which we build our hopes. For this cause, I shall endeavor to offer you some rational evidence of the truth of Christianity as well as full conviction that it is indeed a light shining in a dark place. My first work is to lay the cornerstone of this building and to take a brief prospect of some of those demonstrations of the divine being and perfections which we are so plentifully furnished with from the works of creation and providence. To this end, I have set myself on the words before us as the ground of our present meditations. In these words, we may note:

1. The subject here is the glorious God, where the being and nature of God are expressly considered.

2. The sublime immense nature and glorious perfections of the divine being. The things of God are not only invisible to the bodily eye, but infinitely above the search of the most exalted understanding. For who can by searching find out God? (Job 11:7).

3. The clearest and most infallible certainty of these incomprehensible perfections of God. Though we cannot soar to the interminable heights, or dive to the boundless depths of his infinite nature, we have demonstrative evidence of his eternal power and Godhead with many of his essential perfections. We may be infallibly certain that there is a God, infinite in holiness, justice, goodness, and truth, *etc.*, though we do not know the manner of his existence and operations.

4. The foundation of this certainty, or the means of our obtaining this clear vision of the invisible things of God, is "being understood by the things that are made." We see the cause by the effect and have the brightest evidence that this vast and spacious world, with its amazing magnificence, luster, and harmony, did not proceed from chance, nor could it have been the

product of an author unequal to the work. It must therefore be the workmanship of an infinitely wise and powerful being.

5. The consequence of this evidence, "so that they are without excuse." The heathen world, who know nothing of God but what is visible from the works of creation and providence, may here observe such bright displays of infinite wisdom and power and other divine perfections. Thus, their infidelity is inexcusable. We may sum up the words in this DOCTRINE: *that the glorious being and infinite perfections of God are evidently manifest from the works of creation.*

I shall endeavor to demonstrate this by these following arguments.

I. I think it is unquestionably evident to all men that they themselves have a being. Men do not question their own existence or doubt their being.

II. It is equally certain to every man that he has not always been what he now is. Within the compass of a few years, we were first begotten, conceived, and born and have passed the several stages of time unto the age to which we are now arrived. *Therefore,*

III. It is most sure that we must have our origin from some cause. An effect without an effector, or a real being produced by nothing, is most absurd and the boldest affront to common sense. It is therefore indisputable that we did not make ourselves. For before we had a being, we were nothing and could do nothing. And it is equally certain that we are not the product of blind inactive chance. For how could so noble a being spring out of nothing without any creating power or energy?

From where then do we derive our origin? Not by our parents, they were not omnipotent to command us into being by their powerful word. Nor could such noble, immaterial, thinking substances as our souls proceed from them by way of natural generation. For it is the height of absurdity to suppose that a material substance could give being to a spiritual one. But if it were supposed that even our whole man, soul and body was begotten by our immediate parents, where did they obtain this power? Or from where did their own existence come? If they proceeded in a continued chain of succession from their predecessors, the difficulty remains: where did the first link of this chain originate from? It is as equally absurd to apply self-existence, or self-origination, to the first of our species as to ourselves. This affirms what the psalmist says, "It is he that has made us, and not we ourselves," (Psa. 100:3).

IV. It's also clear that all those other beings which are in the world were produced by some cause. We are not only certain of our own being; but by the same intuitive certainty, we realize the existence of multitudes of other beings beside ourselves. And when we look upward, we see a vast magnificent arch, replenished with innumerable multitudes of bright and glorious orbs, all of them performing their revolutions and discharging their appointed functions with the greatest harmony, beauty, and order. If we look down, we see this huge earth on which we walk, abounding with all varieties of animals and vegetables, each carrying in them the marks of consummate art and skill.

How could we imagine that this immense canopy of the heavens was stretched out, those mighty globes of light hung up in the air and whirled round in their respective circuits, or this earth, with all its furnishings, was created and founded on nothing other than its own sufficiency? Can we, upon the view of a most stately and curious building, overlook the workman that made it by supposing that it just sprang out of nothing or simply constructed itself? No surely! The work shows the workman, and the effect shows the cause.

Hence, the consequence is inevitable, that there is some great and glorious cause not only of ourselves, but of everything we see and know; and this cause is God.

It is for the world to discover the God that created the heavens and stretched them out, that spread forth the earth, that gives breath to the people on it and spirit to them that walk therein, "For the heavens declare the glory of God, and the firmament shows his handiwork," (Psa. 19:1).

I know of only one considerable objection against this reasoning and conclusion that seems worthy of an intelligent mind, and that is this:

The world in all its parts may have eternally existed; all the mutations and revolutions in nature may have been effected by an eternal law or propensity, and all beings in the world continued therefore in an eternal succession.

However, that the world has not eternally existed is evident from the consideration that, had the universe been eternal, it would have been impossible that either the whole, or any part of it, should not have been, or have been otherwise than it is. And if not self-existent, it must derive its being from some cause, and consequently have a beginning. It must also have continued by an infinite and eternal series and succession of necessary causes and effects. For if all the causes and effects in an eternally existing world are not necessary, but contingent, then the world in all its glory and magnificence, in all the symmetry, order, and perfection of its several parts, has forever continued by mere accident, without any cause or reason – which is the height of absurdity. I therefore reassume the former conclusion.

And that is, if the world has had a beginning (as is demonstrated) there must have been some author, some efficient cause, by which it was created and made.

Having discovered the Creator by a view of the creature and found evident demonstration of a divine being from the works of his hands, let us next consider some of those invisible things about him which may be clearly seen and understood by the things that are made.

Firstly, the eternality of God is, without question, evident from the works of creation. We are not capable of a greater certainty of anything than this, that God has existed from eternity.

There cannot be a more unreasonable supposition, nor a more glaring contradiction, than that there was a time in which nothing existed. It would be madness to attribute creating power and energy to mere *nothing*. This consequence therefore forces itself on us, that the cause of all things is an eternal, independent being. From here we may proclaim with the psalmist, "Before the mountains were brought forth, or ever thou had formed the earth and the world: even from everlasting to everlasting thou art God," (Psa. 90:2).

It is likewise demonstrable from the works of creation that this glorious author of all things is a spiritual being. We certainly know that we ourselves are capable of thought, reason, and reflection. And from where do we derive this power? Is it from dead matter? Impossible! For matter is itself utterly incapable of thought and therefore certainly unable to produce a thinking being.

If we allow thought to any matter whatsoever, we must allow it to every particle of matter and by this suppose as many thinking beings as there are atoms in the creation. It would be no less absurd to imagine that some certain composition or modification of matter can produce thought. For unthinking particles of matter, however put together, are matter still; and if there was no thought in any of the parts, there can be none in the whole.

The consequence is therefore inevitable, that since all matter is by nature destitute of thought, our thinking rational souls must derive their being from some immaterial author. It is utterly impossible for that which was produced in the effect to possess what did not first exist in the cause.

And by the same argument, this glorious spirit must eminently have in himself all the perfections of all the innumerable intelligent beings that now are, or ever have been in the world, since they all depend upon him for their beings, capacities, and operations. Is the argument in Psalm 94:9-10 not rational, "He that planted the ear, shall he not hear? He that formed the eye, shall he not see? He that teaches man knowledge, shall not he know?"

If these speculations are too philosophical for some of my hearers, the argument may be proposed in a more easy and familiar manner. It is plain to every observable eye that we have souls as well as bodies, that our more noble part is a thinking, intelligent spirit, that there are and have been multitudes of spiritual beings beside ourselves, and that these all proceed from some cause that is at least equal to the effect, who must therefore himself be a spiritual substance, possessed of all the excellencies of all other spiritual substances in the world. Otherwise, he would have to give what he does not have, and the effect must exceed the virtue of the cause, which is manifestly absurd.

In this way, by a reflection upon our own souls, we have discovered the necessary truth of our Lord's doctrine in John 4:24, that *God is a spirit*.

Let us now go on to consider some of his other divine perfections evident in the book of creation.

It further appears from the things which are made, that the first cause of all things must be an infinite being.

The phenomenal magnitude and amazing extent of the universe loudly proclaim the infinite nature of its glorious author. Though we can have only an imperfect view of this scene of wonders, we may still gaze ourselves into admiration and surprise by what obscure and distant glances we are capable of. If we go no further from home than this globe of earth upon which we dwell, we have here a vast body that measures eight thousand miles in diameter, and above two hundred thousand millions of miles in its bulk or solid content. This must certainly appear to every eye a mass worthy of an infinite Creator.

But as great as this seems, it is (as astronomers inform us) exceeded in magnitude by most of the heavenly bodies and is therefore small in comparison to some of the planets, especially if compared to that stupendous globe of fire, the sun. Now, if we are filled with admiration at the sheer bulk of these huge bodies, how surprisingly great must the space be in which they perform their revolutions! The sun is some 93 million miles from the earth, and much further from some of the other planets which at those vast distances, are all observed to move around the sun, and yet never to interfere, or clash with one another!

Here we might pause to adore the infinite perfections of the glorious author of this spacious system of the sun and planets. But there are yet more distant and greater objects of astonishment that invite our attention, the vast number of stars which fill the spangled canopy and appear innumerable to the naked eye, and yet vastly more numerous when viewed through a telescope, which discovers myriads of them not otherwise visible. Knowing how distant these are one from the other, how immense must be the space which they occupy!

But that is not the end of the mystery. Many astronomers suppose the great multitude of fixed stars to be so many suns, all of them endowed with native light and heat; of like dimensions as our sun and accompanied by a system of planets just as our sun is and consequently occupying as great a space as was formerly supposed in the whole firmament.

This account of the universe makes it appear many thousand times greater than was earlier imagined and should consequently excite our admiration and praises of the glorious Creator and Contriver of such a magnificent world even more so!

But now having long gazed at the phenomenal masses of these heavenly bodies and the immeasurable space possessed by them, it is time to apply these considerations to the present purpose and to see if we can't discover the infiniteness of the Creator from this view of the heavenly regions, which, if we will only open our eyes, must appear in the clearest light. For it is manifest to every observation that the maker, guide, and governor of the universe must be always present in every part of this incomprehensible space. Otherwise, he could not have made, nor otherwise ordered and directed all the parts, operations, and influences of this stately fabric which is impossible to conceive apart from any infinite being.

Besides, he that made the world must also of his free will and choice have ordered and appointed the place of its residence; and nothing but his own pleasure could circumscribe it to these limits or confine it to this space in the boundless void rather than some other. He must therefore himself be equal to all space, whether real or imaginary. That is, he must be an infinite being, whom the heaven, and the heaven of heavens cannot contain (1 Kings 8:27). Here we see the immensity of that glorious being, that, "sits upon the circle of the earth, that stretches out the heavens as a curtain; and spreads them out as a tent to dwell in," (Isa. 40:22).

I might have here spoken to the simplicity and uncompounded nature of God as further evidence of his infinity: but this would be to go out of the way of my text, which confines me to the consideration of the divine perfections as visible in the works of creation; and I think what is said is sufficient.

The unity of the Godhead is also clearly seen from the works which are made. For if there were more gods than one, they could not be infinite. For *two* infinites would be a contradiction. And if finite, they could not be the first cause of all things, as is before demonstrated.

Besides, if there were more than one God, they must all be either supreme, subordinate, or co-ordinate. Two supreme beings are a contradiction in terms. For either one must be superior or both equal, and therefore neither supreme. A subordinate God must be himself dependent and could not have all things depend upon him. In other words, he could not be the Creator nor Upholder of the world. It remains therefore, that if there were a plurality of gods, they must be cooperative, which is equally absurd: for were there several co-ordinate gods, they must either create the world conjointly or separately. And not conjointly, for if they joined together in creating the world, they would all make but one first cause, and each individually being only part of the cause, there could be no perfect being and consequently, no God. Nor could a plurality of gods make the world separately, as there would then be no first cause of all if each caused but a part of the world.

I might further urge the unity of God from his necessary existence. I have already demonstrated that the first cause of all things must be eternally necessary. Nothing can be capable of clearer demonstration. For if there ever had been a time in which God had not existed, he could have had no existence to eternity unless we suppose a cause of the first cause, which is absurd.

Besides, if all things were created by him, he must necessarily be himself uncreated, and being uncreated he must necessarily be eternal. For that which at any time did not exist can never come into being without being created, either by itself or by something else. Now if we suppose God to have created himself, we attribute to him action before existence; which is the grossest absurdity. If we suppose him created by anything else, we suppose a cause of the first cause as before. He must therefore be eternally necessary; and consequently, can be but one.

For if it were possible that the world could be created by one efficient cause (which can't be doubted) there can be but one necessary and primary cause of all things. Everything else must, by default then, be derivative and dependent and therefore can't be primary. Therefore, we can be certain there is but one God, who (as I've already proved) must be the necessary and primary source of all things. As Deuteronomy 6:4 states, "The Lord our God is one Lord." And 1 Corinthians 8:6, "But to us there is but one God the Father, of whom are all things, and we in him."

It is apparent from the works of creation that this glorious God is an omnipotent being. I've already proved that the heavens and the earth, in all their amazing magnificence, curious frame, and regular order, sprung out of nothing at the powerful command of the great Creator. Therefore, since there is an infinite distance between *perfectly nothing* and any *real being* there must be omnipotence employed in this glorious work. The united powers of every finite being would work in vain to create from nothing the most despicable worm, or even a particle of sand. For, as I observed, there is an infinite and eternal opposition between mere nothing and the most inferior creature; and therefore, the vilest insect or smallest particle of dust could not be brought from non-being into being. This is only possible by an omnipotent arm.

And I might further observe that the creation of the world cannot exhaust or be the extent of the Creator's power. For if he once possessed creating skill and ability, he must always retain it; and therefore could (had he pleased) have spent millions of ages in creating new worlds, until their number had exceeded what even the angels could imagine. His omnipotence (had it been his pleasure) could have also created similar worlds in a moment; for there can be no limits to almighty power. As Job 37:22-23 states, "with God is terrible majesty."

The infinite wisdom of the Creator is also clearly manifest from the things that are made. We have already observed that whatever perfection is found in the creature must be first eminently in the Creator. For it's clear that what had its being and beginning from another must have all the properties of its being from the same source. If we apply this to the present case, we shall find it necessary that he who has brought our dust to life and imbued us with so much wisdom must have more wisdom in himself than all the men in the world, since all depend upon him and can have no other ways of knowledge, or extent of power, than what he gives them.

The same may be said with respect to all created wisdom in heaven and earth, which equally flows from the same fountain, who must therefore himself be infinitely wise.

The glorious art observable in the admirable frame of nature likewise loudly proclaims the infinite wisdom of the Creator; while the whole, and every part, do so visibly conspire to answer the great ends of their being. And if we confined our speculations to the most inferior parts of creation only, how many marks of divine skill might be found in the least pebble! What a great variety of shapes, colors, smells, qualities, and uses are there in the smallest herbs or flowers, not to be imitated nor even fully understood by created wisdom! How curiously formed and admirably adapted to their several ends and uses are the most contemptible insects! What industry, conduct, and seeming organized behaviors are found with such inferior a creature as the bee, that even rivals the policy of princes' courts! With what wonderful beauty are the smallest birds and beasts adorned! And with what apparent wisdom do they serve their own preservation and the propagating of their kind! These and similar contemplations sufficiently discover the infinite wisdom that has ordered and does attend and direct all those minute and disregarded aspects of creation.

But if we continue to lift up our eyes to the superior parts of the world, the scene opens further still, convincing our minds of the unsearchable wisdom of God.

How did the parts of the earth come together and not separately fly off into the boundless space? Who has given the sea his decree, bounded it by the shore, and said to its proud waves, "you shall go here and no further?" Who has hung the earth upon nothing and placed it at just the perfect distance from that fiery orb the sun that it is neither scorched and consumed nor made into a continent of ice? Who is the father of the rain or the drops of the dew, by which the earth is watered and replenished? Where do those amazing and innumerable orbs that spangle the sky, placed, and kept at due distances without interfering and dashing together come from? Do not all these, and more wonders of nature than we can count, concur to proclaim that the cause of them all is most assuredly infinite wisdom?

But we need not go so far from home to find the truth we are seeking. If we merely consider our bodies, how wonderfully are they made! What astonishing art and skill appears in the variety of the parts, in their beauty, symmetry, and proportion, their connection, dependence, and use! Who can search out the wonders of this frame, or fully account for so much as the motion of a leg or finger? But if we reflect upon the wonderful operations and faculties of the mind, our surprise grows all the more. The nature of the soul with its powers of understanding, memory, will, *etc.*, are beyond our search. Well may these and similar reflections strike us with astonishment.

And there is doubtless vastly superior evidence of art and skill in creation which we know nothing of. We can but join with the psalmist in his holy admiration of these things in Psa. 104:24, "O Lord, how manifold are thy works: in wisdom hast thou made them all!"

What has been said clearly portrays the divine omniscience and shows us plainly that he that made, he that directs and governs this magnificent world with such order and regularity, must have all things present and future in his view at once.

Otherwise, he could not have contrived and disposed all the innumerable parts with such admirable glory and surprising harmony. And if his omniscient eyes did not inspect every atom of creation and clearly behold the darkest recesses of nature, it would be impossible that his providence could take care of the whole world, even to its minutest parts, as we see it does. How else could they all subsist? As Psalm 147:5 states, "Great is our Lord, and of great power, his understanding is infinite."

In this I might clearly prove that the author of all created goodness, whether natural or moral, is himself infinitely good; that the fountain of all created justice, is himself infinitely just; that he whose nature is highest perfection, cannot be charged with any defect and must therefore be infinitely holy; and that he who has made, so carefully preserves, and bountifully provides for all creatures and all creation is himself infinite mercy and love. But the time would fail me to particularly insist upon these things; and these and the like consequences, are so natural and easy from what has been already observed that they don't require insistence or proof.

I shall therefore now hasten to some practical inferences from the doctrine.

If there is a God of such infinite perfections, it is a natural inference that he should be worshiped in a manner agreeable to his glorious nature.

This is a truth so plainly legible in the law of nature that the most barbarous heathen and salvage pagans have always assented to it; and it is even impossible for a rational mind to refuse an assent. Can we consider him as the author both of our essence and subsistence, as the fountain of all our mercies and comforts, upon whom we depend, in whom we live, and unto whom we are beholden for all things, and yet suppose we owe him no reverence or homage? Doesn't even nature itself teach us to look to the rock from whence we are hewn? "A son honors his father, and a servant his master; if then he be a Father, where is his honor? If he be a master, where is his fear?" (Mal. 1:6).

We are hereby instructed to manifest our dependence upon God by praying to him. If our life and breath are at his disposal, if all the good we want or hope for is treasured up in him and must flow from him, the very first principles of reason will teach us to run to him for our every need.

It is a rational acknowledgment of the fountain of our mercies to look to him for all our good and to receive all as coming from his bountiful hand. This is an acknowledgment that a parent expects from his children and a prince from his subjects. How much more may the eternal majesty expect it from such vile worms and indigent creatures as we. We should therefore come to him with a deep impression of our own nothingness. For what are such clods of animated dust, compared to the immense fountain of all glorious perfections?

We should come to him, with a humble sense of our natural unworthiness. For we are but clay in the hands of the sovereign potter and can therefore have no claim of favor from him. We must come to him with a humble resignation and submission to his will, for he is an eternal Sovereign, and we are at his absolute and uncontrollable disposal.

The ends of this proposed duty of prayer are not to give God a new acquaintance with our circumstances and necessities nor to make any change in his counsels. No! There can be nothing hidden from the flaming eye of his omniscience. And concerning his counsel, he is in one mind, and who can turn him? What his soul desires, this he does. But we should pray to him that we may be ourselves fit recipients of his mercy. Prayer is a direct means to keep us humble and to deepen our love for him from whom we implore and obtain all our good, and to incline us to live to him as we derive life from him.

The fact that prayer has a direct tendency to excite and enliven our religious contemplations and affections is self-evident. And it is plainly obvious to every man's reason that he is not qualified to receive mercy that forgets both his God and his own soul, that regards neither the bounty nor the Benefactor, and that will in no way testify his dependence upon God nor his subjection to him. The very light of nature does therefore preach that doctrine, as Psalm 95:6-7 declares, "O! Come let us worship and bow down, let us kneel before the Lord our maker. For he is our God, and we are the people of his pasture, and the sheep of his hands."

If we deny that the glorious nature of God is so highly exalted above such poor worms of the dust as we, that we are too inferior creatures to be the objects of his care and regard, we insinuate that an omniscient, omnipresent, and infinitely perfect being, who without any pains or difficulty, inspects and orders every atom in the creation, takes care of every worm and fly, arrays the lilies of the field with their beautiful clothing, and provides food even for the ravens of the valley. If there were anything, any creature or aspect of creation below his notice, from where could it subsist? What could uphold it in being, or prevent its return to its original causes?

From what has been said, it further appears that we should not only manifest our dependence upon God by praying to him, but our gratitude by thanksgiving and praise. That gratitude is a natural debt to a benefactor, and that our thankfulness should be proportioned to the benefits received, are truths acknowledged everywhere. Should not our hearts and mouths be forever filled with praises to the infinite fountain of goodness, from where so many streams of mercy are continually flowing to us, and from whom we are continually receiving such a variety and affluence of what is fit for our use, comfort, support, ornament, and delight?

Besides the wonders of redeeming love and the mercies which refer to another life, the good things of this world which we all enjoy give us cause to raise our grateful praise in the language of Psalm 103:1-2, "Bless the Lord, o my soul, and all that is within me, bless his holy name. Bless the Lord, o my soul, and forget not all his benefits."

I might further observe here that the consideration of his divine perfections should make us most serious, hearty, sincere, and spiritual in all our religious devotions. It is most evident that this omniscient eye cannot be flattered and deceived with any formal demonstrations and superficial pretenses; for he knows our thoughts afar off, searches our hearts and reins; and has clearest views of our most inward motions and retirements of soul.

To conclude, this doctrine teaches us that we are utterly indebted to this glorious God. Horror accompanies the very thought of being at odds with this dreadful majesty who has made us, preserves us, and can crush us in pieces in a moment or fill us with unutterable anguish at his pleasure. It would be better for us that the whole creation should conspire our misery and ruin than that the God who made us should refuse to have mercy on us, and the Rock that formed us should show us no favor. For if God is for us, who can be against us? (Rom. 8:31). It is therefore a case worthy of our most earnest endeavors to determine the means of obtaining the favor of such a God.

A Demonstration of the Apostate State of Man by Nature, and of the Glorious Provision Made for His Recovery by Jesus Christ

Romans 5:6, "For when we were yet without strength, in due time Christ died for the ungodly."

Having now demonstrated the being and infinite perfections of God, and from there our extreme necessity of an interest in his favor, I am now to investigate the way and means of becoming favorites of this glorious majesty. We will also consider whether we are naturally on good terms with him, and if not, whether he has made any provision for our reconciliation and reobtaining his lost favor. Both of these considerations offer themselves in a manner worthy of the divine nature, and agreeable to human reason, in the words before us in Romans 5:6, where we may note firstly, the fallen, apostate state of mankind, which is that Christ died for the ungodly. That is, he died for those who were in a state of enmity and opposition to him.

The text indeed gives us no light into the cause of this guilt and woe. But reason as well as revelation plainly dictates that it is inconsistent with the merciful nature of our glorious Creator and natural Lord, either to create us in an estate of sin and misery or to reduce us to those wretched circumstances without just provocation. Therefore, our rebellion and apostacy must necessarily be the source of this corruption, as we shall more particularly consider.

Secondly, we may note the awful consequences of our apostacy. We were without strength. The original word here rendered "without strength" is very emphatic and represents that we are in the most languishing, helpless, and distressed of circumstances. It alludes to and is taken from the state of those that are brought to the brink of the grave by some grave sickness.

Thirdly, we may note the remedy provided for this distress and the means of our recovery from this languishing helpless state, which is that Christ died for us. When all human help failed, and we might have utterly despaired of recovery by any created power, the glorious son of God stepped in to rescue us and purchased our deliverance with his own blood.

Fourthly, we may note the seasonable nature of this remedy provided for us. In due time Christ died, *etc.* Which must either refer to the time pre-ordained of God for this glorious deliverance, as some understand the words, or rather simply to the fitness of the season when our blessed redeemer undertook and accomplished our ransom.

The misery of the world at the time of Christ's appearing, evidenced by the universal depravation and deluge of idolatry that covered the face of the earth, makes it appear to have been a fit season for the glorifying of his divine compassion. And the union of the nations under an imperial government also made it a fit season to proclaim the salvation procured for them.

But for a more distinct handling of the words, I shall consider them as consisting of these two propositions:

I. That mankind is brought into a sinful, miserable, helpless state.

II. That our Lord Jesus Christ did in due time die for their deliverance out of this state.

The method I propose to expound these propositions is to distinctly show that they are not only revealed truths but are also most agreeable to the light of reason. And then as I pass along, make some brief reflections by way of improvement.

Proposition I. That mankind is brought into a sinful, miserable, and helpless state.

This may be illustrated by first offering some rational evidence of this awful truth and then by inquiring into the cause or reason of it.

For evidencing the truth of the proposition, I shall offer these following considerations.

1. It is plain to every intelligent mind that a rational creature may sin against God.

Everyone must acknowledge that our glorious Creator sustains a near relation to us as our common parent and the author of our being, on which account he justly claims our love and reverence. Further, he has an absolute sovereignty and dominion over us as our Lord and King, by which he is entitled to our subjection and obedience. If instead of that love and reverence which we owe our heavenly Father, we disesteem his infinite perfections, or if instead of that obedience which is due this glorious King we do those things which we know to be contrary to his will, we violate the first laws of nature and sin against God. This is a plain case and is without defense.

The only difficulty before us is how we shall know what the will of God is concerning us. If there is no law, there can be no transgression; and if God has given us no manifestation of his will, he can't expect or require our obedience.

In answer to this objection, I must not take it for granted that the scriptures are a divine revelation; that is yet to be proved. But we must consider whether we cannot by the light of nature discover such manifestations of God's will and our duty that will render our nonconformity to it *criminal* and *sinful*.

And if we merely contemplate the perfections of the divine nature, this will appear in the clearest light. For whatever is contrary to any of them must be displeasing to God and repulsive to his will. To demonstrate this, the light of nature enjoins the belief of one God alone and thereby teaches us that he is the only object of proper divine and religious worship. Consequently, it is a violation of the law of nature to worship other gods, or that any idol of our imagination should be esteemed, loved, trusted, obeyed, or honored as God.

Moreover, our own reason dictates to us that God is himself infinite righteousness and justice, and therefore, that every act of injustice whether it respects God or man as its immediate object is contrary to his nature and will. Likewise, God appears to the eye of reason as a being of infinite goodness and mercy. And any imitation of this divine perfection in beneficence, mercy, love, and charity is acceptable in his sight, while bitterness, wrath, hatred, cruelty, or any acts of unkindness are as contrary to his will as they are to his merciful nature.

By a particular reflection on these attributes, much of our duty towards God and man might be discovered. And by surveying his other perfections, we might find further acquaintance with his will concerning us as well as further evidence that we are capable of sinning against him.

What man will teach his neighbor that treachery, fraud, and violence are sinless and innocent? What parent will instruct his eldest son that he may innocently, if he can secretly, take away his life to possess his estate? What prince will teach his subjects that they are under no religious bond to obedience, but may without sinning against God, turn rebels and traitors? If man is under no duty to God, and if nothing we can do is sin against him, what a creature would man be, and what a hell would earth be!

It is rather most evident that there are such things in nature as virtue and vice, right and wrong. This is what our own consciences continually demonstrate, and what all nations have always agreed in. In this way, it appears agreeable to the very first dictates of reason in Gen. 4:7, "If you do well, shall you not be accepted? And if you do not do well, sin lies at the door."

2. We all have a sad experience, that our first and chief inclinations are to those ways that are most repugnant to the holiness of the divine nature; and to that righteousness that God reasonably expects from us.

As soon as we are capable of action, the leading affections and passions of the mind are irregular and vicious, the appetite exorbitant, and the whole bent of our soul is after what is most opposite to our duty and happiness. So much so that if our youth was without restraint and we were allowed to resort to our natural inclinations, we should be authors of destruction to ourselves and to one another. With what diligence and vigilance must the poison sprouts of vice and immorality be weeded up, to prevent our headlong progress in impiety towards God and man!

We begin our course, and then in our more advanced age, what battles does every thinking person find taking place between his reason and passions, by which he is even distracted with this perpetual struggle and contest for victory! With what difficulty do we form our minds to any reverence of our glorious Creator, or conformity to his justice, goodness, or holiness! How difficult a task is it to regulate our appetites, or to hold the reins of our inordinate inclinations and desires!

This is what the heathen world have observed in themselves to be agreeable to that of the apostle, "the good I know, I do not; and when I would do good, evil is present with me." These things lie open to every observer, that the, "imaginations of the thoughts of their hearts are only evil continually," (Gen. 6:5).

3. We cannot help but observe that the greatest part of the world, against the light of their own reason, live in sin against God and in disobedience to him.

How many people bow down to sticks and stones, worship the host of heaven, or lie prostrate at the altars of some vile pagan gods while forgetting the God that made them and the rock that formed them! And though custom or lack of education may cloud their understanding as to satisfy their minds in this stupid idolatry, their own reason should show them the sin and folly of worshipping and serving the creature more than the Creator, who is blessed forever.

And besides this superstition and idolatry by which the greater majority of mankind dishonor *the eternal majesty*, how does sinful lust and passion overtake reason and principle, even in the most enlightened parts of the world? What of all the malice and envy, the luxury, riot and excess, the sinful and sensual pursuits, that most of the world are chargeable with? Can the perpetrators of such gross desires plead ignorance? They sin against light and against their own reason and conscience. As Romans 1:21 states, "Because that, when they knew God, they glorified him not as God, neither were thankful; but became vain in their imaginations, and their foolish heart was darkened."

4. It is evident that this gravitation to sin flows from the corruption and pollution of our natures. For where can such corrupt streams proceed but from a polluted fountain? And where can such wickedness come from but a wicked and depraved nature? What reason can be given for why men chase risky, sinful pleasures rather than those that are innocent and rational? They gratify their lusts at the expanse of their comfort, health, reputation, estates, and everything else that is pleasant and precious. And why do they rush on in their sinful and irrational courses, against contrary convictions, against all restraints, divine and human? What can be the cause of all this, but the depravity of our natures and the cursed enmity of our hearts to God and all that is good?

Though we need no other argument to give us full assurance of this sad truth, yet a particular view of the faculties, habits, and dispositions of our souls would give us further evidence that our hearts are *deceitful above all things and desperately wicked*, (Jer. 17:9).

5. This state of sin and pollution which we find ourselves in must necessarily be a state of guilt and woe.

Sin in its formal nature is directly repulsive to all the properties and perfections of God and is the highest affront and indignity to him. It is as much a contempt and denial of his propriety in us and dominion over us as it is a refusal to be subject to his known will.

Sin is a contempt of his goodness and mercy when we choose base and brutish pleasures before his favor. And our refusal to be drawn to him and his service by all the sweet attractions of his gracious providence is a horrid reality and a gross disregard of his omniscience and omnipresence, that we dare sin in his presence and act contrary to him when we know that our actions are open before him. It is a daring defiance of his omnipotence for such worms as we are to oppose him, as though we can make our case good against the God who made the world and can make us fuel to his flaming vengeance at his pleasure. It is a vile contempt of his holiness and purity when we prefer the pollutions of our own sinful appetites before his righteous nature. In a word, it is a contempt of all his attributes and direct enmity and rebellion against him.

From this contemplation, it is most apparent that we wretchedly deviate from the great end of our creation, both by the habits and acts of sin. For it is the height of stupidity to imagine that infinite wisdom should make so noble a being for no higher purposes than to show contempt for his attributes, spurn his authority, and maintain a course of opposition to him. And the same consideration lays open before us the guilt of a sinful state. For if rebellion and treason against an earthly sovereign is considered evil and treasonous so as to involve the rebel in deepest guilt and expose him to the sharpest revenges, how much more criminal and guilty must the man be who maintains a rebellion against the king of kings, and lives in a course of open enmity and defiance both to his being and government!

What kind or degrees of punishment an offended sovereign will inflict upon such rebels is not so easily discovered by the light of nature. But that we are justly exposed to punishment is visible from the nature of our crimes. None question the equity of punishment awarded to traitors; how much less we can reasonably expect to escape unpunished for our treason against heaven!

If it is just for man to punish the delinquent, it must necessarily be so for God to do, who is the fountain of all created justice and whose holy nature is the only pattern for our virtues and honorable conduct. It is therefore only reasonable to expect that those who prefer the ways and fruits of sin to the favor of God should be left to their unhappy choice and be shut out of his favor forever. They may not, they cannot suppose that such guilty and polluted creatures, these enemies to God and holiness, should be the objects of divine love and complacency or be admitted to the favorable presence and delightful blessing of a holy God. No! For he is of purer eyes than to behold evil or to look upon sin with approval.

In this way, we see that the loss of God's favor and by this the loss of all happiness (which can only consist in his favor) is the natural and necessary result of our state of sin and enmity to him. And though we cannot discover by natural light to what manner or measure of positive penalties our sins expose us, yet we have the greatest reason to expect and fear terrible manifestations of God's righteous displeasure.

And if some objection is presented that is contrary, in that it seems by observation that the most wicked and profane are often in happy and flourishing circumstances, while the more holy and virtuous are under the greatest afflictions as though they were the chosen objects of God's wrath, then I answer that this objection only confirms the considerations before us. For no matter how dark and inexplicable the present dispensations of providence may be, God is a God of justice; and the judge of all the earth will do right.

So, we can naturally conclude from the present seeming inequality in God's dealings with us that this life is not the place of rewards and punishments, but that there will be future retribution in which these crooked things will be made straight, and the flourishing prosperity of wicked men will appear to be but a preparation for their ruin and a fattening period before their slaughter.

We may also reasonably conclude that God will, whether at first or at last, reconcile the justice and equality of all his dispensations. And since this does not appear from the present period of providence, we may look for a future season, for the manifestation of his just response to sin and sinners and for the execution of his deserved wrath upon them.

That we are made for a future state will appear from the contemplation of our own natures. Here we may certainly find that we have spiritual and immaterial substances within us (as I have fully demonstrated in a former discourse) and that our souls, being immaterial, must be likewise incorruptible and therefore naturally immortal, made to survive their earthly tabernacles, and to continue to live and act when our bodies return to the dust from when they came.

Now can it be imagined that God has made so superior a creature as man, endowed him with a rational and immortal soul and with such elevations of mind, only to act a short while in this world to just propagate his kind and then return him to an eternal state of insensibility and inactivity? Surely not! These low views of who God created us to be are altogether unworthy of infinite wisdom. It is therefore evident from the immortal nature of our souls, and from the short amount of time we are in this world, that we are here in a state of probation. We are, in fact, candidates for another world where we are likely to meet with the rewards of our present behavior, whatever it is.

In this way, we discover our guilty miserable state by sin, that God is angry with the wicked every day, (Psa. 7:11), and that there is destruction awaiting the wicked and a severe punishment set aside for the workers of iniquity, (Job 31:3).

6. It is certain that we are naturally helpless and without strength or skill to recover ourselves out of this plunge.

We see ourselves in the pit but can't find the way out by our own power or wisdom. We have a woeful experience, our nature is polluted, and all our faculties are depraved. Our passions rebel against our reason, and we are continually sinning against God and provoking him to anger. So how can we conquer our lusts, regulate our affections, and get reconciled to God?

Here let the deist try his skill. Let him without the assistance of revelation draw up a perfect system of the laws of nature. Let him consult the means of restoring our lost innocence and of keeping our affections and passions under the government of religion and reason. Let him call in the help of all the philosophers of Greece and Rome for his assistance in this arduous undertaking. And in the conclusion, he'll have nothing but his labor for his pains while he continues in the same inexplainable labyrinth.

This is apparent from the fruitless pains of all the wisest moral heathen in this case who, though knowledgeable of our depravity and misery, could never find out the cause nor cure. They have indeed, at least some of them, given excellent moral rules for the government and moral conduct of human life. But what light have any, or all of them given, in terms of this present inquiry? What remedy have any of their schools of thought proposed for our misery? What means do they possess to restore to reason the empire of the mind and to reduce the exorbitant passions and appetites? What way have they conceived to shake off our guilt and to re-obtain divine favor? Here they have run themselves out of breath to no purpose, while every sect has proposed a contrary, or different scheme; and all have left the difficulty as they found it. And had all human wisdom been collected into one head, the case would have been the same. "For we are all as an unclean thing, and our collective righteousness is as filthy rags, and we do fade as a leaf; and our iniquities like the wind, have taken us away," (Isa. 64:6).

Having thus discovered our misery, we may next consider the cause of it. How is it that mankind is brought into such a sinful, miserable, and helpless state?

To which I answer,

1. We could not at first come out of the hands of our holy Creator, in such a corrupt, polluted, and sinful state.

Had God at first created us in this state of defilement, he must have taken pleasure in our sin and pollution; and where then would have been his holiness? Had he at first made us with a natural necessity of being guilty and criminal, he must have been the author, as well as punisher of our guilt. Where then would have been his justice? Or had he been the original and necessary cause of our misery, where would have been his goodness and mercy? Therefore, to suppose God to be the author of that nest of sin and uncleanness that lies in our wicked hearts, the cause of our vile affections, ungovernable passions, and exorbitant appetites, as well as the fountain of all these poison streams, is to attribute to him worse than the worst of human affections. It is implicitly to say that he made us on purpose that he might delight himself in our misery. Such shocking blasphemy must be far from every imagination. Therefore, it appears that, as Ecclesiastes 7:29 states, "God made man upright, though we have sought out many inventions."

Therefore,

2. The state that we find ourselves in makes the account of this matter in the third chapter of Genesis most probable.

I shall not now concern myself with the debate as to whether this story is to be literally or allegorically understood. Either way, it is a natural and rational supposition that our first parents, through the power of temptation, were guilty of disobedience against God. And by this both for themselves and their posterity, they lost the innocence and happiness of their first state.

It appears very likely from the consideration of our present degeneracy, that we are the branches of a corrupt stock and the offspring of rebellious parents. And though we may meet with some difficulty in reconciling the imputation of original sin to the holiness and justice of God, this serves our present purpose and clears up the consideration now before us. It is not difficult to suppose that God should punish an ungrateful rebel with the loss of all his original excellencies and perfections, both of body and mind. And it is a natural and familiar supposition, that a degenerate stock will have degenerate branches; that the offspring will be like the parent; and that the streams partake of the nature and qualities of the fountain.

Besides, God may justly impute the sin of Adam to his offspring as (1) we were all seminally in our first parents, and in that sense partakers with them in their transgression. And (2) that they acted as our public representatives, and therefore were to stand or fall for us, as well as themselves.

With these two considerations the difficulty vanishes. And I see nothing in the nature of the thing that can make it unbelievable where God as an absolute sovereign should constitute Adam the moral and natural head of all his posterity to represent and act for them all in what he did. We don't consider it unusual in our temporal affairs to be equally obliged by what our representatives who act in our name and stead do, as if they were our own personal actions. Nor should we in this present case have thought it unjust to have partaken of the blessed fruits of Adam's obedience, had he stood. On what basis then can we complain of the imputation of his disobedience in us?

After all, whether we can thoroughly reconcile this matter to our own ways of thinking or not, we can't find a more probable reason of our lost miserable circumstances, than that by *one man* sin entered the world, and *death* by sin, as we are told in Romans 5:12.

But whatever is the cause, we cannot doubt the malady. We have too sad an experience of our misery to call that into question: and since we see the house on fire, it does not so much concern us to anxiously determine by what means the flame was kindled as to consult a method to extinguish it.

The difference here being that it is of infinite importance for us to search for some way of obtaining a pardon for our sins, a sanctification of our natures, and a reconciliation unto God. Our present state is not to be continued in. It is a dreadful condition to be God's enemy; a fearful thing to fall into the hands of the living God. And where shall we run for help? From what corner shall we look for deliverance from the miseries we feel or fear? Will pagan religion afford us relief? We have already heard that the best schemes of their wisest sages have been utterly insufficient to this purpose.

And a thinking person will hardly be persuaded that the worship of a herd of vile deities, with rites as vile and detestable as the gods themselves, should please such an eternal majesty who will not give his glory to another nor his praise to graven images.

Shall we consult our oracles of wisdom and wit and seek some rational scheme of religion and happiness from our modern pagans, the deists? These libertines can vainly boast of unprejudiced reason and science, as though wisdom must die with them. They can put out the eyes of conscience, and bravely scoff at revealed religion as an idle dream and the effect of a melancholy imagination or enthusiasm. But which of them has ever pretended to propose a method of obtaining inward peace and purity, happiness here and salvation hereafter?

In this way, so far our search has been vain and fruitless. And we are miserable indeed if we can find no end to our quest, no religion to trust in, no foundation to fix upon.

Let us then examine the Christian religion and see if there is not more reasonable answers to be found there, whether that has made any adequate provisions for the recovery of fallen man and for securing our present and future happiness. Our consideration of this answer immediately brings us to the second proposition:

Proposition II. Our Lord Jesus Christ did in due time die for the deliverance of sinful man out of his miserable and helpless state.

The glorious and eternal son of God beholding our apostate and perishing state, looked down with divine compassion upon a miserable world, deluged in sin and guilt, and undertook their ransom. And that God might be just, in the pardon and justification of sinners, he has become their surety; so that by his bearing the punishment due for their sins, he might atone offended justice, and by his representative righteousness he might purchase for them glory and happiness.

How is this glorious mediator qualified for this great undertaking? In the truth that he is the eternal God, so the dignity of his person might give sufficient merit to his obedience. And he likewise became man, like us, so that he might be able to suffer the penalty due our sins, and that satisfaction might be given to justice by the same nature that offended it. He was moreover both God *and* man, that by representing both parties at odds, he might mediate between them. And since death, in the largest significance of the word, our almighty Savior has for our sakes, and in our stead, encountered this king of terrors in his most terrible appearance, in all his pomp, with all his darts and poison. In this way he tasted death for men and *redeemed us to God* with his own blood.

This is summarily the meaning of the words of our text and of the proposition before us. And if this doctrine is true, it reflects a glorious light into our dark minds, plucks us out of the jaws of despair, and proposes a happy means of life and peace. It is therefore well worth our while to distinctly consider the veracity of the Christian institution and see whether its precious and comfortable doctrines may be confided in.

In order that I may assist you in this inquiry, I shall at present offer you some strong probabilities on the side of Christianity. And then (if God permit) in some future discourses to that purpose, I will offer you full, plain, and undeniable evidence of these blessed truths.

The strong probabilities that I would now take notice of, may be proposed under these two considerations.

I. That the Christian revelation, if true, is every way worthy of God.

II. That it also, in every way, answers the miserable circumstances of fallen man.

Let us first consider that the Christian revelation is every way worthy of God.

This consideration, if fully pursued, might show us how all the divine attributes and perfections most gloriously harmonize and shine forth with brightest luster in this our salvation by Jesus Christ. But the time before us will allow only some very brief hints on this subject. However, I would willingly say enough to establish you in the present truth and assist your contemplations on this delightful theme.

This way of salvation appears worthy of God in that in this was a glorious manifestation and illustration of infinite goodness, mercy, and love. An eternity is not long enough to admire, adore, and praise the surprising wonders of redeeming love. For if we consider the objects of such a mercy – poor apostate rebels – there could be no motive but divine compassion for mercy to replace justice in the deliverance of such criminals from deserved wrath.

If we consider the freeness of this love, it will appear infinite like the glorious fountain of it. If we consider the nature of that salvation thus secured for us, and that it contains not only a freedom from sin and guilt but a title to God's favor and to an eternal state of glory and happiness, we may with just admiration cry out, "what is man that thou art mindful of him?"

If we consider the author and price of this salvation, that God so loved the world as to give his dear son for us, and has redeemed us with his own blood, our amazement increases, and mercy appears in its highest exaltation. All these considerations together, with the many others that might be proposed, give us cause with ravished souls to acknowledge that the breadth, and length, and depth, and height of the love of God in Christ passes knowledge! (Eph. 3:18).

The magnificent display of infinite justice in our redemption by Christ makes it also appear worthy of God. Were justice swallowed up of mercy (as it must have been had God saved sinners without a just and satisfactory substitute), we might reject the doctrine as unworthy of an infinitely just and holy God. But he has shown himself relentless in his demands of satisfaction by requiring the last bit of the surety due from the principal debtor and by punishing his own dear son with such a horrific, bitter death as the sinner's representative. "He is the Rock, his work is perfect: for all his ways are judgment: a God of truth and without iniquity, just and right is he," (Deut. 32:4).

If it is objected that it cannot be just to transfer the punishment from the guilty to the innocent, then I answer that God by right of his supreme jurisdiction, might relax the law and transfer the penalty. And though justice requires full satisfaction, he might in absolute sovereignty, accept it from a *surety*.

It is true indeed that the Redeemer, as he was the Lord from heaven, was not liable to any constraint or compulsion to do this. But I see nothing either in the nature or law of God that should make it unjust to accept full satisfaction from him when voluntarily offered.

I acknowledge that it would be unjust among men to accept the life of an innocent for a guilty person, because we do not have jurisdiction over the disposal of our own lives. But our Lord had in himself the power to lay down his own life, and the power to take it up again.

But I must hasten to observe that the most glorious manifestation of God's holiness and purity in this work of our redemption makes it likely to be a divine plan. Nothing could provide a greater discovery of God's relentless opposition to sin than the amazing sufferings of his own dear Son. This demonstrates sin to be a weight that even infinite mercy could not bear, in that the blood of his well-beloved son must be the only sacrifice to appease his displeasure against it; and that he could without relenting, behold the bitter agonies of him with whom he was well pleased when he was made sin for us. This shows us that he is glorious in holiness.

The omnipotence of God likewise appears in its highest perfection in this glorious work. God's creating the world out of nothing, and his upholding and governing all things by the word of his power, are not greater evidence of omnipotence than our redemption by his incarnate son. The incarnation of Christ, and the union of the divine nature with the human, is such a miracle of power that it exceeds all finite thoughts of the highest order. And the same almighty agent is discovered in our Lord's miraculous conception of a virgin, in the triumphs of his cross, and the victory over all our spiritual enemies obtained by his death, resurrection from the grave, and ascension into heaven. In a word, the whole transaction of our salvation by Christ is a manifestation of omnipotent grace.

The glories of the divine wisdom do also shine forth with brightest splendor in the work of redemption. The very projection of this plan was beyond the capacity of any finite understanding. The method (though most reasonable and agreeable) is so deep and mysterious that it could not have been the product of human invention. This consideration alone is enough to convince us of the divine origin of the Christian institution. The end of this grand divine plan – to exalt God's glory and restore man's happiness – was worthy of infinite counsel; and the means of accomplishing this vast design could be adjusted only by God himself.

Such infinite wisdom! How unsearchable the counsel that took occasion from our sin, which was the highest opposition to divine perfections, to make all his attributes shine forth with brighter glory. And in so doing, not only to bring infinite mercy and inflexible justice into the sweetest harmony, but to manifest both in the greatest luster, the one in punishing the sin and the other in pardoning and saving the sinner! Who but God could have found the means for mercy and truth thus to meet together, and righteousness and peace to kiss each other?

And we may still with greater admiration adore the miraculous plan for reconciling God and man by uniting the infinitely distant natures into one person and thereby ordaining such a mediator who by partaking of both natures, is interested in both parties. And so, in every way he was fit to reconcile God to man and man to God! But I must not continue in this grand subject which would take a large volume to significantly consider it and a whole eternity in the just admiration of it. The brief glance we have already had into this contemplation makes it appear that God has in this abounded towards us in all wisdom and prudence, (Eph. 1:8).

Now that I have with all brevity considered how the Christian revelation is worthy of God, I will now observe:

II. That in every way it answers the miserable circumstances of fallen man.

What could be more agreeable to the perishing circumstances of guilty condemned sinners than the joyful tidings of pardon and salvation, of a deliverance from the depths of woe, and a title to joy unspeakable and full of glory upon such easy and honorable terms?

This justly recommends the Christian religion above all others that ever were or could be contrived.

And if we take a view of the tenor and properties of this institution, we shall find it is so adapted to the nature of man, to his various stations and relations in the world as well as to his comfort here and happiness hereafter, that no other religion could ever claim similar ground on these accounts. So, this above all others appears to be of *divine* origin.

The doctrines of the gospel are all holy and spiritual, agreeable to the ennobled nature and faculties of our souls. The precepts are most just and reasonable, directly tending to make us holy and happy, charitable and beneficent. The motives are most noble and sublime, sufficient to work upon our affections and passions, to deter us from sin and enflame our desires after the reward of holiness. And here the vices of pride, worldliness, and sensuality, of injustice, fraud, persecution or oppression, fierceness, or impatience, are justly condemned and prohibited. And a flaming sword brandished before us, to prevent our commission of these and such like sins. Here we are taught self-denial, justice and mercy, brotherly love, unity, peace, and kindness one to another with the most endearing attraction to a blessed life. Here we also have most excellent rules for order and government in the world and for the peace and stability of kingdoms and commonwealths. Here we may find the choicest support for all the troubles and afflictions we can conflict with, and even against the fears and terrors of death itself.

Here we have all rational pleasure and satisfaction indulged us. Here may our minds be spiritualized and exalted to the highest elevation they are capable of in this life, and yet raised with expectations of higher perfections in the world to come. In a word, the grand divine plan of redemption is in every way perfect for human nature and designed for our present and future happiness; and is therefore worthy to be esteemed the wisdom of God and the power of God, (1 Cor. 1:18).

I must now conclude this discourse with some brief practical inferences.

I. We have cause with raised affections to adore and praise the infinite mercy of God for revealing this glorious salvation to us in the gospel.

Life and immortality were purchased by the obedience of Christ, but they are brought to light by the gospel. And it would have been as well for us to have had no salvation purchased as none revealed. In both cases a thick cloud of despair covered our souls that we could never have seen through. But now from the distinguishing mercy of God, the sun of righteousness has *arisen upon us*; and the Day Spring from on high has visited us. The Light of life blazes into our souls. And the way to heaven like the path of the just, is as a shining light, that shines more and more unto the perfect day. We are under the happiest advantages possible, to secure an interest in this Savior and a title to the glories that will be revealed!

Let us consider how great a part of the world are yet groping in thick darkness, utterly losing their way in the mists of ignorance and error, without God, without Christ, and without hope in the world. And yet the grace of God that brings salvation, having appeared to us, causes us to be lifted to heaven by our privileges. And it will surely appear that this special favor calls for special thankfulness and loudly summons all the faculties of our souls to be closely engaged in that inquiry. "What shall I render to the Lord, for all these benefits towards me?" (Psa. 116:12).

And if we yet further consider how unworthy we are of such discriminating favor, it will give us cause to reflect on these divine obligations with a rapture of soul. Had there been anything in us that could have been any incentive to this distinguishing mercy, it would have lessened the obligation: but there was nothing in us, more than in the darkest regions of the earth, to move God's compassion to us or to excite him to make known to us the riches of the glory of this mystery among the Gentiles. Free sovereign grace alone deserves the praise. And our ingratitude will be of the blackest dye, if these reflections don't make the fire burn in our breasts and inspire us with continual praise and thankful resoundings of such special and signal mercies.

II. Let us be exhorted to make it our conscientious concern to obtain an interest in this salvation that was in such a wonderful way provided for us and so freely tendered to us.

Let us with flaming ardor of soul, and with most undeniable insistence, wrestle with God for an interest in Christ by faith; that he may become of God to us, wisdom, righteousness, sanctification, and redemption, so that we through him may be heirs to an inheritance with the saints in light.

We should be ultimately careful that we don't perish from under the gospel, lest this magnify our guilt and aggravate our future condemnation, that *light* is come into the world, and we chose darkness rather than light.

A Demonstration of the Christian Religion from the Prophesies of the Old Testament

Luke 24:44, "And he said unto them, these are the words which I spoke unto you while I was yet with you; that all things must be fulfilled, which were written in the law of Moses, and in the prophets, and in the psalms concerning me."

Having in our last discourse considered our apostate and miserable circumstances, and the hopes of recovery from this state of sin and guilt by our Lord Jesus Christ, I am now to add to the strong probabilities then urge some full and clear demonstrations of this precious truth, that *God has so loved the world, that he gave his only begotten Son, that whosoever believeth in him, should not perish, but have everlasting life.*

For proof, I shall first consider the clear evidence of this doctrine from the prophecies of Christ in the Old Testament, and then show you how it is ratified by God himself with the great seal of heaven by the miracles performed by Christ and then by others in his name. This proof falls under present consideration from the words of our text in which we may note:

Something supposed and taken for granted, *i.e.*, that the Scriptures of the Old Testament prophesied of

Christ, that the Messiah was written of in the law of Moses, in the prophets, and in the psalms, which expressions, according to the Jewish mode of speaking, include all the sacred and canonical books of the Old Testament.

This was a truth universally received among the Jews both before and at the time of our Lord's incarnation, such that it needed neither illustration nor confirmation.

We note the divine authority and undoubted veracity of these prophecies of Christ; they must all be fulfilled.

These sacred prophecies being the oracles of God, are founded on his truth and faithfulness and are as immutable as God himself and, therefore, will be fully accomplished.

For a clearer understanding of the words before us, we may note the end and design of our glorious Lord in this argument, which was to confirm and establish the faith of his disciples in himself, as the hope of Israel and the Savior of the world.

This appears from the connection of these words with the foregoing context. In the 37th verse, we find the disciples terrified with our Lord's miraculous appearance among them, supposing they had seen a spirit. And we are told in the 41st verse that their surprise not only continued but was accompanied with incredulity and unbelief. Our Lord, to obviate both their difficulties, first takes meat and eats before them, to convince them that he was *not* a spirit; and then urges the present argument as sufficient forever to silence all their doubts about the cause of his sufferings and his resurrection from the dead. This argument he had before instilled in them, and now again leaves with them, as a standing confirmation of their faith in that important article. The sum of which argument is this, that all the sacred writings (which could not fail being accomplished) unanimously predicted the manner of life, the death, and resurrection of the Messiah. Therefore, they could have no room left for surprise with relation to him in whom they had seen the accomplishment of all these prophecies, as this was an attestation from God himself of his divine mission.

We may sum up the words of this doctrine in this way, that *the fulfillment of the Old Testament prophecies concerning our Lord Jesus Christ are a sure evidence that he is the Messiah.*

For the illustration of this observation, I shall endeavor to show:

I. What a prophecy is.

II. How a prophecy may be said to be fulfilled.

III. That there were prophecies of Christ in the Old Testament which are fulfilled.

IV. That the accomplishment of these prophecies is sure evidence that Christ is the Messiah.

I. What is a prophecy?

In this consideration I mean to briefly show in what sense it is to be understood in the present argument. And as it affects the case before us, I understand a prophecy to be *a divine prediction of future contingent events*. I call it a divine prediction because it's the sole prerogative of omniscience to foresee future contingencies. It is not within the compass of any finite understanding to foretell those things that have no foundation in nature, nor dependence on natural causes.

And I consider contingent events as the only object of prophecy because it requires no prophetic spirit to predict those events that are in themselves necessary, or that depend upon the nature of things.

But I need not insist upon this description, the case being plain, familiar, and universally agreed in,

II. To consider how a prophecy may be said to be fulfilled.

1. A prophecy is sometimes said to be fulfilled by way of accommodation only. When a prediction of one thing may by reason of some similitude between them be aptly connected to another.

In this sense, the word "fulfilled" was in frequent use among the Jews who, when speaking scripturally, would frequently mention the fulfilling of scripture when they meant no more by it than an agreement of circumstances between the case considered and the quoted text; or an example parallel to something foretold or spoken of in scripture.

In this allegorical sense, the sacred penmen of the New Testament also sometimes speak of the fulfilling of prophecy where there is no direct or literal accomplishment, nothing but an agreement or accommodation of the event and prediction. In this way, our Lord's return from Egypt is said to be that it might be fulfilled that was spoken of the Lord by the prophet, saying, "out of Egypt have I called my son," (Matt. 2:15). And thus, the destruction of the young children by Herod is said to be a fulfilling of that which was spoken of by Jeremiah the prophet, saying, "In Rama was a voice heard, lamentation, and weeping, and great mourning, Rachel weeping for her children," *etc*. Whereas it is evident that the first cited words of the prophet immediately refer to the deliverance of the children of Israel from their Egyptian bondage, and the latter to their distress and anguish from the Babylonian carnage and captivity.

From this use of the word fulfilled, our modern infidels have, unreasonably enough, taken occasion to insinuate the weakness or unfaithfulness of the evangelical historians. But was there anything more common among the most famous Greek orators than to adorn their discourses with quotes taken from Homer, Euripides, or some other of their poets when they never intended, nor could their auditors understand anything more than a bare citation to the matter treated? Or is there anything more common among us than to cite scriptures in this allusive manner, which have no direct or immediate reference to the subject matter of the discourse? And I must tell them that to continue in their infidelity even after full and clear evidences of the truth of Christianity have been from time to time offered them, that there is fulfilled in them what was spoken by the prophet Jeremiah 5:21, "they are a foolish people, and without understanding, which have eyes and see not, which have ears and hear not," though I don't think the prophet had those in mind when he spoke those words.

2. A prophecy is more strictly and properly fulfilled when a prediction, according to its direct meaning and primary design and intention, meets with an exact and full accomplishment.

3. And a prophecy may be said to be fulfilled when it has a double accomplishment; and is completed both in the type and anti-type, that is, both in the sign and the thing signified.

It has been questioned by very learned and judicious men whether any prophecies may in strictness of speech be said to have such a double reference. They rather suppose that those prophecies that have been so understood look unto Christ and him only. But then it must be acknowledged that there is a sudden transition from some other person or thing to the Messiah, and that two different events are predicted in the same continued discourse. One example is that prophecy in 2 Samuel 8:12, 16 that was fulfilled both in Solomon, and in one *greater* than Solomon.

Another is the promise to David in verse 12 that when his days were fulfilled and he should sleep with his fathers, God would set up his seed after him that should proceed out of his bowels and establish his kingdom.

This was literally verified in Solomon. But then the promise in the 16th verse that his house and kingdom should be established *forever*, and that his throne should be established forever could not ultimately terminate in Solomon but rather pointed to a more stable and durable reign than his, even to an everlasting dominion which shall not pass away and to a kingdom which shall not be destroyed. In this sense the psalmist understands this promise, "His seed shall endure forever, and his throne as the sun before me. It shall be established forever as the moon, and as a faithful witness in heaven," (Psa. 89:36-37). And agreeably from this prophecy, the tradition universally embraced among the Jews that the Messiah must be the son of David, which interpretation we see justified by the event.

Next, I proceed to observe:

III. That there were prophecies of our Lord Jesus Christ in the Old Testament, which are strictly, literally, and exactly fulfilled.

The time before us will not allow that I should enter into a distinct consideration of the multiplied prophecies of the Messiah found everywhere in the Old Testament to show how they are verified in Christ. I shall therefore only consider four or five of those that exactly point out the time of our Lord's coming, and then just take a cursory view of some of those predictions that describe the circumstances of his appearing.

I begin with the blessing of dying Jacob to his son Judah in Genesis 49:10, "The scepter shall not depart from Judah, nor a lawgiver from between his feet, until Shiloh come; and unto him shall the gathering of the people be." It is generally believed, even by the Jews themselves, that Shiloh here refers to the Messiah, though there is not such a joint agreement among interpreters.

And yet I cannot see that there was any other scepter promised to Judah in the 10th verse than to Dan in the 16th verse of this same chapter. The difference between them consisted not in the formal nature of their government or dominion, but in the duration or continuance of it. They each had, according to this prophecy, their princes, rulers, judges, or heads of their tribes for a long time after, even until the captivity of the ten tribes when Dan lost his scepter.

And if this interpretation is allowed to me, (and I cannot see why it should not be), it is obvious to every eye that this famous prophecy has had a literal and full accomplishment. The scepter never departed from Judah until the coming of Christ. Even in the time of the Babylonian captivity, they had their lawgivers from between their feet; they were allowed the use of their own laws even when removed from their own land, as appears from Esther 3:8, "And Haman said unto Ahasuerus, there is a certain people scattered abroad and dispersed among the people, in all the provinces of thy kingdom; and their laws are diverse from all people, neither keep they the king's laws."

But how soon after the incarnation of our blessed Savior did Judah lose all authority when both their civil and ecclesiastical state were utterly subverted!

And are not we ourselves, as well as the other Christian nations, happy evidence of the gathering the people unto this predicted Shiloh, according to the prophecy before us? In this way, we have blazing evidence that the patriarch Jacob did foresee Christ's day, and that this prediction is punctually and exactly verified in our glorious Savior.

I shall now proceed to the consideration of another prophecy, which likewise precisely points out the time of the Messiah's manifestation. It is that in Daniel 9:24-26, "seventy weeks are determined upon thy people, and upon thy holy city; to finish transgression, and to make an end of sin, and to make reconciliation for iniquity, and to bring in everlasting righteousness, and to seal up the vision and prophecy, and to anoint the most holy. Know therefore, and understand, that from the going forth of the commandment to restore and to build Jerusalem, unto Messiah the prince, shall be seven weeks and threescore and two weeks. The streets shall be built again and the walls, even in troublous times. And after threescore and two weeks, shall messiah be cut off; but not for himself. And the people of the prince that shall come, shall destroy the city and sanctuary; and the end thereof shall be with a flood; and unto the end of the war, desolations are determined."

Here is a plain prediction, that within the space of seventy prophetical weeks, or weeks of years (that is 490 years, as the Jewish rabbis themselves expound it), the great things determined upon the Jewish people and the holy city, should be accomplished, transgression finished, reconciliation made for iniquity, everlasting righteousness brought in, the vision and prophecy sealed up, and the most holy anointed. And within seven weeks and sixty-two weeks (that is 483 years) after the going forth of the commandment to restore and to build Jerusalem, the Messiah should appear, and be cut off, but not for himself. And that after his death, the city and sanctuary should be destroyed, and the people given up to desolations. Now everyone skilled in chronology may see a most exact accomplishment of this prophecy.

Though we do not have an express direction when to begin the seventy weeks, or 490 years when all those transactions relating to the Messiah were to be accomplished, we are plainly told that the sixty-nine weeks, or 483 years, were to begin with the going forth of the commandment to restore or to build Jerusalem and to terminate at the death of the Messiah. And if we begin counting in the twentieth year of Artaxerxes Longimanus and end on the thirty-third year after Christ, the year of his death, then the event corresponded exactly to the prophecy, as to the time of his manifestation and crucifixion. And were not the predicted consequences of his coming also most exactly fulfilled? Did not the Romans destroy the city and sanctuary and bring the determined flood of war and desolations on the Jewish state?

Another prophecy, which foretells the time of our Savior's appearing may be found in Haggai 2:7, 9, "And I will shake all nations; and the desire of all nations shall come; and I will fill this house with glory, saith the Lord of hosts. The glory of this latter house shall be greater than of the former, saith the Lord of hosts; and in this place will I give peace, saith the Lord of hosts."

These words consist of a threefold prediction: (1) the convulsions and confusions that all nations were to be exercised with, (2) the appearance of the desire of all nations in rebuilding the temple and that it should exceed the former temple in glory, and (3) the peace that will be consequential to the manifestation of the prince of peace.

Now as to the first, none acquainted with history is ignorant of the accomplishment of it by the ravages and devastations made in the world by Alexander the Great and his followers, by the perpetual bloody wars and desolations that continued in the four kingdoms that succeeded to, and stood up in the place of the great horn of that rough goat; and by the Romans, whose conquering sword at last brought them all into subjection.

And then, how soon after the end of this concussion of the nations, did the desire of all nations come into the temple and by his sacred presence, make that house more glorious than the former, though it was in everything else inferior to it! And as to the last of these predictions, how exactly was it fulfilled in the peaceable reign of Augustus, wherein all nations seemed to have forgotten their former fierceness and rage, as well as the use of their military armor!

Thus, we are irresistibly constrained to acknowledge the accomplishment of this prophecy in our Lord Jesus Christ, by his coming at the very time here foretold, immediately after the shaking of all nations and during the continuance of the second temple, and in that remarkable time of universal peace.

A fourth famous prediction of the time of our Lord's incarnation is that in Malachi 3:1, "Behold, I will send my messenger, and he shall prepare the way before me: and the Lord, whom ye seek, shall suddenly come to his temple; even the messenger of the covenant, whom ye delight in. Behold, he shall come, saith the Lord of hosts."

That this prophecy related to the Messiah is clearly manifest by the titles and epithets here given him, "the Lord whom ye seek," "the messenger of the covenant whom ye delight in." And that it was fulfilled in our Lord Jesus Christ is equally manifest by his appearing in the temple before the destruction of it, after the messenger, John the Baptist, was sent to prepare his way by baptizing, preaching repentance, and warning the people to believe in him that should come after him. But this is so plain that I need not insist upon it.

I might here also reference Nebuchadnezzar's dream in Daniel 2:31-46 as a prophetic indication of the time of the Messiah's appearing by which is foretold that after the expiration of the third, and during the fourth monarchy, a stone should be cut out of the mountain without hands, that should break the fourth (the Roman) monarchy to pieces, and become a great mountain that shall fill the whole earth; or as the prophet expounds it, a kingdom that shall never be moved. The exact verification of this prophecy is too obvious to escape the notice of any observer. Anyone who knows even just a bit of Roman history cannot deny that our Lord appeared in the height and glory of that empire; and that after his advent, the fourth monarchy did gradually wane away until it was utterly subverted by the inundation of the goths and vandals and that this stone, against all opposition from that kingdom of iron, has grown to a great mountain and will (as we may surely conclude from this prophecy) in his own time, fill the whole earth.

Before I proceed to the consideration of other prophecies of our blessed Savior, I would here take liberty to observe that not only the Jews, but all the neighboring nations, about the time of Christ's coming, entertained raised expectations of some glorious monarch that should bring great revolutions upon the world. And where should they derive these notions from, or from where should they form these expectations, but from these cited prophecies?

Now let us return to the consideration of some other prophecies that predict the circumstances and consequences of our Lord's appearing.

It was foretold that the Messiah should be born of a virgin (Isa. 7:14), in the town of Bethlehem (Micah 5:2). That he should reside in Galilee, and particularly in Zebulon and Naphtali (Isa. 9:1). That he should enter Jerusalem upon an ass, and a colt the foul of an ass (Zech. 9:9). That by his miraculous operations, the eyes of the blind should be opened, and the ears of the deaf unstopped, the lame restored to the use of their limbs, and the dumb to their speech (Isa. 35:5-6). That he should appear in low, mean, and afflicted circumstances, be despised and rejected of the Jews, be a man of sorrows and acquainted with grief (Isa. 53:2-3). That he should finally be cut off, but not for himself (Dan. 9:26). And the circumstances of his death were likewise foretold by the prophets. And I need not tell you from the evangelical historians how all these circumstances of his life and death were exactly fulfilled in our Lord Christ.

And as to the consequence of Messiah's coming, it was prophesied that after his death, the Jewish sacrifices and oblations should cease, and their holy city and sanctuary would be destroyed (Dan. 9:26-27). That he should bring forth judgment to the Gentiles, who should come to his light and see his righteousness and glory (Isa. 42:1-2, 40:3), which were so visibly accomplished in cutting off the natural branches of the olive tree, and grafting the Gentiles into the same stock, that it must be willful blindness not to see it.

In truth, there is scarcely any passage of the birth, life, sufferings, death, resurrection, ascension, or glory of our Savior, or scarce any circumstance of the state of his kingdom here in the world but what are particularly prophesied of in the Old Testament. But the time will not allow, nor does the case require, that I should enlarge upon this further. I therefore proceed to consider:

IV. That the accomplishment of these prophecies is sure evidence that Jesus Christ is the Messiah.

I confess indeed, that the accomplishment of some single prophecies in our Lord Jesus Christ is not convincing proof that he was necessarily the person predicted and pointed out by them. There were (for example) many others, beside Jesus of Nazareth in Judea, before the scepter departed from Judah, who descended from the tribe of Judah, from the loins of Abraham and David, were born at Bethlehem when the Messiah was to be expected, *etc*. But then the united accomplishment of all these prophecies in our blessed Lord renders the evidence clear and incontestable, that the prophecies of the Messiah in the prophets belonged to him and him alone.

Only Christ could claim to have descended from Abraham, from Judah and David; of appearing just 483 years after the decree for building and restoring Jerusalem; of being born of a virgin, in the town of

Bethlehem; of working so many miracles; of dying and rising again; of setting up a spiritual kingdom, where the Gentiles should be subjected; and all the many other prophetic descriptions of his person and government, too many to be recounted here, which all point to our Lord Jesus, and therefore (as I observed) prove him to be the Messiah. This will be plainly demonstrated if we consider,

1. That the accomplishment of these prophecies is a clear and certain indication of their divine origin.

Finite understandings can have no means of foreknowledge. But either from the nature and reason of things, or by inspiration from him who has all things present and to come in his omniscient eye, their eyes can be opened to see. By one of these means therefore all the events we have been considering must have been foretold, or else they would have been imagined. Mere conjecture would not explain them, for in all the face of nature what can you find that resembles an incarnate God? Or what could account for even the obscurest hints of the time, manner, and consequences of his manifestation? They could not have been an imposter, for that would not justify the event. We see them fulfilled and for that reason ascertain that they were prophetically foretold. We see that God himself acknowledges the prophecy by its completion, which he would not have done if these prophecies had come from those attempting to deceive. The consequence therefore irresistibly forces itself on us, that these were the oracles of God. It is a just challenge and a reasonable argument in Isaiah 41:22-23, "Let them bring forth and show us what shall happen. Let them show the former things what they be, that we may consider them; and know the latter end of them: or declare us things for to come. Show the things that are to come hereafter, that we may know that ye are gods."

I know of one objection that can with any evidence be offered against this arguing, which is, that God may, for the trial or punishment of a people, let the devil have limited space into some of his future purposes. But even in these cases, God is still the author and the power in control, though the devil is the communicator of these prophecies. God is the only entity with the power to bring forth the event, even when Balaam is the prophet. He who adjusts all future things in his own breast, and whose sovereign pleasure and purpose make them possible, can only foresee what, how, or when they shall be. To ascribe a foreknowledge of future contingencies to the devil is to place him on God's throne and to give him the glory of divine perfections. But I proceed to consider,

2. That it is here necessary that all the attributions of Christ in all the divine prophecies are true since God can neither deceive nor be deceived.

The accomplishment of these prophecies reveals their glorious author, along with his necessary truth and faithfulness. If they are of divine origin, they have a divine truth and can no more be chargeable with falsehood or mistake in any instance, than God can deny or contradict himself.

In this way, we have the strongest and most unquestionable assurance from the holy prophets that our Lord Jesus Christ, whom they have foreseen and of whom they have so particularly foretold, is the wonderful counsellor, the mighty God, the everlasting Father, the prince of peace. He is God's own Son, *God in the flesh*, "Immanuel," God with us, the Lord our righteousness and the salvation of the ends of the earth. In a word, all things are fulfilled that were written in the law of Moses, the prophets, and the psalms concerning him.

I am aware that ancient objections may urge against all this, saying these prophecies were all written since the event and as such are rather histories of what is past than predictions of things to come. But this is impossible, as the sacred books were kept in the hands of the bitterest enemies of Christianity (the Jews) whose malice against Christ would not have allowed them (had they even been capable) to have conspired in such a forgery and interpolation.

Can it be imagined that they would have devised these prophecies on purpose to have brought a perpetual infamy upon themselves? Could they in this way frame weapons against their religion, and study the confusion of their own faces! Besides, even if they had been willing, they would not have been able to have imposed such upon the world. Had it been possible that all the Jews in the world, in their most distant dispersions, should have to a man come together in this undertaking; had they corrupted all their Bibles and not left one copy to detect the fraud (which is unreasonable enough to suppose as this blessed book was in the hands of multitudes beside them). As well, everyone in every place the text was dispersed among the Gentiles, especially in the Greek translation of it, would also have been in on the conspiracy, if any such thing had been done. In a word, the world would have had to conspire in this cursed imposture, and no copy of the Bible be left to expose the villain, nor any man know how, why, or when it was done. Any such idea is completely ludicrous.

I. We therefore learn, that as the foregoing prophecies of the Messiah are all fulfilled in our Lord Jesus Christ, they are a clear and sound testimony from heaven that he is the predicted Savior of the world. So, likewise, is the completion of his own predictions an attestation to and confirmation of his heavenly mission.

The Messiah was foretold to be a prophet like unto Moses, whom we should hear in all things (Deut. 18:15). And our blessed Jesus justified his claim to that character by his many prophecies of future things, which have been so punctually verified. He discovered the most secret thoughts of men's hearts, foretelling the treason of Judas while he was yet in his inner circle and perhaps before it was conceived even in Judas' mind. He also particularly foretold his own death, with the specific manner and circumstances of it, the time of his continuance in the grave, his resurrection, and his glorious ascension. He promised to the apostles and others the gifts of the Holy Spirit with his miraculous powers and operations. He predicted the destruction of Jerusalem and the utter abolition of the temple along with the preludes of that desolation. And I need not be particular in demonstrating the exact accomplishment of all these prophecies, nor do I have time to consider the many prophecies in the New Testament received from him and spoken in his name.

I will therefore select only one from among them, the verification of which is at this time visible to all the world: the prediction of anti-Christ, whose coming was foretold to be after the downfall of the Roman empire when that could no longer restrain his tyranny (2 Thess. 2:7). The manner of his coming was to be with pride and arrogance, exalting himself above all that is called God; and yet under the guise of a minister of religion, sitting in the temple of God, strengthening his interest by all power, and signs, and lying wonders (2 Thess. 2:4, 11). The place of his residence was to be in a great city, built upon seven mountains. The city of Rome only answers this description (Rev. 17:9, 18). His reign was to be tyrannical with horrible persecution of the saints (Rev. 13:7 and elsewhere).

Who can help but see an exact accomplishment of these and many other characters of anti-Christ in the pope and Roman papacy, and thereby a full evidence of our Savior's omniscience in foretelling these events?

II. Here we are instructed in the divine authority of the sacred scriptures.

The spirit of prophecy, which everywhere appears in them, must necessarily be the Spirit of God, who alone can be the author of a true prophecy.

The Old Testament has this attestation to its truth and divine origin, it being throughout a continued series of accomplished prophecy. A great part of that blessed book consists either of more direct, clear, and express, or more dark and allusive predictions of the hope of Israel and salvation by Christ.

Besides the more explicit prophecies of this great salvation interspersed through almost every book of the Old Testament, what were all the whole mosaic institution, with the Levitical priesthood, rites, and ceremonies, especially their sacrifices and bloody oblations, but types and shadows of our blessed Savior, to keep alive their faith, hope, and desire of his salvation before his coming? There are indeed some historical parts of this holy book that are not properly prophetical; but these have also their reference to Christ, and not only represent God's care, guidance, and government of his church but also show us his faithfulness in securing the promised seed in the promised line and in preserving the tribes in their entirety, that our Lord's descent might be, as was promised, from the loins of Abraham, the tribe of Judah, and the family of David.

In this way was a large part of the Old Testament an index to point out the person of Christ, with the time, manner, end, and consequences of his manifestation. And the full and bright accomplishment of all these things is not only a verification of the promises and prophecies but a declaration from heaven that these scriptures were given by inspiration of God.

I might here also, as further evidence that the Old Testament is indeed the Word of God, consider the many other prophecies that had no special reference to Christ. Such were the predictions of the vast numbers of Abraham's posterity, the children of Israel's sojourning in Egypt as well as the duration of their bondage there, their deliverance, return to Canaan, and their flourishing circumstances during their obedience in that happy land. Such were the predictions of the destruction of the ten tribes, the Babylonian captivity and the term of its duration, the circumstances of the Jews after their return, their desolation and dispersion, and their rejection of Christ. There were also numerous prophecies relating to persons, kingdoms, or countries, as well as the prophetic description of the four successive monarchies and of the state of the world during the reign of each of them. There are, as you know, accomplished prophecies of this kind everywhere in the scriptures and, as such, innumerable evidences that those holy books were the dictates of God himself.

The New Testament has likewise sure confirmation of its truth and divinity, not only by the multiplied prophecies contained in it, many of which are already fulfilled and some are yet to be expected. But also, by the predictions of this new dispensation in the Old Testament. The Old Testament foretold the coming and kingdom of the Messiah; the New Testament assures us that he is come and has erected his spiritual kingdom, as was predicted of him. The Old Testament dispensation consisted of many types, shadows, and mystical ceremonies; the New Testament shows us how they were completed and fulfilled in Christ, the substance of them all. The Old Testament describes the time, circumstances, and manner of this new dispensation; the New Testament in every way answers the description, as a copy of the original or the face a well-drawn picture, in all the parts.

Thus, we see the Old Testament illustrated by the New, and the New confirmed by the Old, and both contrived by infinite wisdom. For is it possible that any created understanding could devise and foresee so many and various representations of Christ and his kingdom of grace, all agreeing with the event, at such a distance from their completion? Surely not! This would exceed the foresight of every created intelligence. Is it possible that the religion should not be of God, which has been predicted and confirmed by a successive series of prophecy from the very earliest ages, and joyfully beheld through the prospective glass of the promises by all the faithful since man's first apostacy? No certainly!

III. Therefore, from the accomplishment of past prophecies we have the greatest assurance that those, yet future, shall be also fulfilled. For they all have the same glorious author; all depend upon the same power and veracity.

From these we may entertain certain expectations of that flourishing state of the church, when anti-Christ shall be destroyed by the spirit of Christ's mouth and the brightness of his coming; when the fullness of the Gentiles shall be brought in and all Israel shall be saved. At this time Christ shall have the heathen for his inheritance, and the uttermost parts of the earth for his possession; and the kingdoms of the earth shall become the kingdoms of the Lord and of his Christ.

At this time, impenitent sinners may surely expect a swift approach of their dreadful and eternal woe. They may justly entertain trembling expectations of the accomplishment of those terrible predictions, of indignation and wrath, tribulation and anguish; of fire and brimstone and horrible tempest for their part in the lake which burns with fire and brimstone which is the second death.

These truths allow believers to lay down their heads in the dust with comfort, under the blessed prospect of Christ's glorious appearing, when their vile bodies will be changed to be like his glorious body. They will then receive that glorious reward, which when he comes, he will bring with him. They may with courage encounter the king of terrors and pass through the dark valley of the shadow of death, keeping their promised inheritance in view, looking to that blessed hope and the glorious appearing of the great God and our Savior Jesus Christ. They may joyfully make this echo to the promise of his coming, even so, come Lord Jesus, come quickly. Amen.

A Demonstration of the Christian Religion from the Miracles Performed by our Lord Jesus Christ, both Before and After His Crucifixion

Acts 2:22, "Ye men of Israel, hear these words: Jesus of Nazareth, a man approved of God among you, by miracles, and wonders, and signs, which God did by him in the midst of you; as ye yourselves also know."

These words of our text directly lead us to the consideration of the last evidence proposed for confirmation of the divine mission of our blessed Savior. They were successfully urged by the Apostle Peter as an irrefutable argument of this important truth; and if duly considered, cannot fail to yield for us also a full and complete conviction of it.

For the right understanding of these words, we may note in them,

1. A declaration of a matter of fact, that God did work miracles and wonders and signs by Jesus of Nazareth.

The apostle here considers our Lord Jesus Christ in his human nature only, as he appeared to the Jews and was by their wicked hands crucified and slain. As he was considered a man by them, he could not be the author of these miraculous operations. So, these miracles, wonders, and signs are justly ascribed to deity as the sole efficient, though not exclusive of Christ as the second person in the Godhead, but only as he was Jesus of Nazareth, or the man Christ Jesus.

2. We may note the end and design of this declaration, which was to convince the audience that our Lord Jesus Christ was by these miracles approved of God. "Ye men of Israel, hear these words: Jesus of Nazareth, a man approved of God among you, by miracles," *etc*. Peter here takes the advantage of a vast concourse of people, convened from all quarters to the feast of Pentecost, to preach a crucified Savior. And by irresistible arguments, to convince them that Jesus of Nazareth was *indeed* the expected Messiah. This he evidences, first by the accomplishment of prophecy, now surprisingly visible to them all, in the gift of tongues that were newly conferred on the apostles and company. And then, as a concluding argument, he urges the miracles of our Lord as a declaration from God himself of his heavenly calling, and as a testimony from heaven, that the same Jesus whom they crucified was sent, authorized, and approved of God, and by him constituted both Lord and Christ.

3. We may note an appeal to the auditors themselves, as witnesses of the facts alleged, "as ye yourselves also know." The argument was founded upon matters of fact; and was therefore more or less forceable, according to the truth or falsehood, notoriety, or uncertainty of the facts on which it depended. If they

were false or uncertain, the conclusion drawn from them must be very precarious; if true and publicly known, it must be most just and necessary. The apostle therefore concludes the argument with these words, thereby intimating that it must necessarily be of irresistible force to them, who were themselves spectators of these miracles. But we may more particularly consider the argument in speaking to this doctrine, that the miracles performed by our Lord Jesus Christ are a full and clear evidence that he was approved of God and had his mission from him.

In speaking to this doctrine, I propose this method:

I. To consider what a miracle is.

II. To prove, that there were real miracles wrought by our Lord Jesus Christ.

III. To make it appear that these miracles are full and clear evidence of Christ's divine mission, and that he was the promised Messiah.

I. Consider what a miracle is.

In terms of explaining the nature of a miracle in the common theological sense of the word, a miracle has been ordinarily described as an extraordinary operation of God in nature, either stopping its course, or producing some effects that are above its laws and power. And it has been the received doctrine of divines, that the working of miracles is the sole prerogative of God himself. But some very learned men who have lately written on this subject have justly found fault with this description. They make it evident that a true miracle may be wrought by angels. They therefore choose to define a miracle as a work effected in a manner unusual, or different from the common and regular method of providence, by the interposition either of God himself or of some intelligent agent superior to man for proof or evidence of some doctrine or in attestation to the authority of some particular person.

And yet there were certainly miraculous works performed by our blessed Lord that exceeded the powers of all the angels of light. So rather, let us consider miracles as extraordinary and immediate operations of God in producing effects, either contrary to, or different from the common course of nature and providence. I call them extraordinary and immediate operations of God, exclusive of all finite power, while allowing that angels may be able to work some true miracles. Yet there are many of those operations that are as much the prerogative of God himself over his creation.

I further describe miracles to be effects contrary to, or different from the common course of nature and providence. For though the power of God is as much discovered in the ordinary works of nature and providence as in those effects that are most contrary to, or different from their common course, yet those only that are extraordinary are properly miraculous, as they are evidences that God suspends the common motions of nature for some uncommon or extraordinary purpose.

II. Real miracles were performed by our Lord Jesus Christ.

This is fully confirmed by the following considerations:

1. The sacred writers report that many such miracles were wrought by our blessed Savior.

It would take up more than all the time before us to particularly consider all these demonstrations of his mercy and power recorded in the scriptures. And yet their number doubtless far exceeded the particular account of them. I shall therefore select a few (and I need mention but a few) of those indisputable instances of the miraculous works performed by our Lord Jesus, both before his death and after his resurrection, and recorded in the sacred writings.

We read in the beginning of John 2 where Jesus honored a wedding with his presence and manifested the glory of his omnipotence by turning water into wine better than the natural blood of the grape. Now though it is possible that created spirits might invisibly remove the water and substitute wine in the place of it, yet the historian plainly intimates that this was immediately done by our Lord's powerful word, and that it therefore was no less than that which a creating power could possibly effect.

A like instance was when he fed five thousand men, besides women and children, with five loaves and two fishes, and four thousand men, besides women and children, with seven loaves and a few little fishes, and causing the bread to increase by being eaten and the fragments to exceed the quantity of the loaves at first set before the multitudes (Matt. 14:19, 15:34). It might be easily supposed that an angel could have invisibly brought a fresh supply of bread and fish in the place of what was eaten. Yet the sacred story represents it as Christ's own immediate work and therefore as a clear manifestation of his omnipotent power.

Equal evidence of his immediate and omnipotent agency was when he forced the elements to acknowledge their sovereign Lord, and the wind and sea to cease their tempestuous arguing and to become calm and quiet at his word (Mark 4:39).

I might add to this his curing so many diseases without any visible means but his own powerful word. And the multiplied instances of his casting out devils, and even forcing the unclean spirits themselves to acknowledge and proclaim him the Son of God (Matt. 8:29).

But if any should choose to believe that all these instances were due to the agency of created spirits, there are others yet to be considered that certainly exceeded the utmost stretch of angelic power, such as his giving life to the dead, commanding departed souls to return to their bodies by the same powerful word by which they at first had their being. Thus, he raised Jairus' daughter to life to the astonishment of all who were in the house (Mark 5:38-41). He stops the parade of mourners carrying the widow of Nain's son to the grave and delivers him alive to his sorrowful mother (Luke 7:14-15). He speaks life into Lazarus that had been dead for four days and was now corrupting in his grave (John 11:43-44). I might here also add the testimony born to his heavenly mission by the resurrection of many at the time of his crucifixion (Matt. 27:52-53). Though it is not expressly told us that these were raised by his power, yet their resurrection was plainly accomplished as a direct response to his sacred character and an express declaration from heaven that he was truly the Son of God.

But the greatest miracle of all was his own resurrection from the grave, which he assures us was performed by his own power (John 10:18). This truth is the greatest evidence of his omnipotence in that God would never have justified a false pretender and impostor by raising him from the dead. Here we have therefore a plain declaration from God himself that Jesus Christ our Lord is the son of God by his resurrection from the dead.

Upon the whole, it appears plain to me that all the angels in heaven or devils in hell could not break the bars of the pit asunder, summon the dead from their graves, and cause them to reassume life and action. This must be the work of him alone who holds the keys of life and death in his hands.

But even if all these mentioned miracles had been performed by the interposition of angels, they nevertheless are God's seal to justify Christ's person and render his commission authentic. They were at least extraordinary works of providence in justification of our Lord's person and doctrine and were therefore a testimony from him who governs all the wheels of providence.

It is true, that if these wonderful works were the agency of created spirits, they would not agree to the description of miracles upon which I proposed to establish the present argument. But there were also multitudes of miraculous operations, professedly performed in the name and by the power of our Lord Jesus Christ, that do not nor cannot lie open to any exception and in which we have all the assurance of God's immediate agency.

What I refer to are the miraculous gifts of the Holy Spirit, conferred not only on the apostles and other officers in the church, but upon many (if not upon all) true believers, at the beginning of the gospel dispensation. The excellent author of *Miscellanea Sacra* handled this subject with such strength and fluency as to give infidelity a fatal wound and lay it gasping at his feet. What I now propose is to just give you a few hints from that admirable author to convince you that God has born witness to Christianity, not only with signs and wonders and diverse miracles (such as we have already discussed) but also with these gifts of the Holy Ghost.

Joel prophesies in Joel 2:28, "And it shall come to pass afterward, that I will pour out my spirit upon all flesh; and your sons and your daughters shall prophesy, your old men shall dream dreams, your young men shall see visions; and also upon the servants, and upon the handmaids in those days, will I pour out my spirit." And John the Baptist, Christ's forerunner, bare record, "I saw the Spirit descending from heaven like a dove; and it abode upon him; and I knew him not; but he that sent me to baptize with water, the same said unto me, upon whom thou shalt see the spirit descending, the same is he which baptizes with the Holy Ghost," (John 1:32-33). The material part of which record the three other evangelists give us: thus, Matthew says of John the Baptist, "I indeed baptize you with water unto repentance; but he that cometh after me, is mightier than I, whose shoes I am not worthy to bear; he shall baptize you with the Holy Ghost and with fire," (Matt. 3:11, Mark 1:8, Luke 3:16). But when should this be? Not while tabernacling here in the flesh, but after his ascension to the Father; as he himself assures his disciples in John 14:12, "Verily, verily, I say unto you, he that believeth in me, the works that I do, shall he do also; and greater works than these shall he do; because I go to my Father." And verse 16, "And I will pray the Father, and he shall give you another comforter that he may abide with you forever." Verse 26, "But the Comforter, which is the Holy Ghost, whom the Father will send in my name, he shall teach you all things; and bring all things to your remembrance, whatsoever I have said unto you." Our Savior adds in 16:7, "Nevertheless I tell you the truth, it is expedient for you that I go away: for if I go not away, the comforter will not come unto you: but if I depart, I will send him unto you."

And after our Lord's resurrection, he renews the same promise to them in Luke 24:49, "And behold, I send the promise of my Father upon you; but tarry ye in the city of Jerusalem, until ye be endued with power from on high." And Acts 1:4-5, "And being assembled together with them, commanded them that they should not depart from Jerusalem: but wait for the promise of the Father which ye have heard of me. For John truly baptized with water; but ye shall be baptized with the holy ghost, not many days hence." (See also Mark 16:17 and John 20:22).

Now that we have seen the prediction and promise of the gifts of the Holy Ghost, let us next consider the accomplishment of these prophecies which will appear in the clearest and strongest light by reflecting upon the representation of this matter in the Acts and epistles.

These gifts of the Spirit were communicated in two different ways, either immediately by the Holy Spirit falling upon them, or mediately, by the laying on of the apostles' hands. Those who received the Holy Ghost in the former way were said to be baptized with the Holy Ghost, to have him poured out upon them; or to be filled or anointed with the Holy Spirit. (See Acts 11:15-16, 2:23, 4:31, 10:38.) And probably none ever received the Holy Spirit in this immediate way without the visible symbol of cloven tongues like fire. When the Holy Spirit did not so visibly descend, but was communicated by the laying on of hands, it is called the giving and receiving of the Holy Spirit (Acts 8:15-19), the ministering of the Spirit (Gal. 3:5) and imparting spiritual gifts (Rom. 1:11). I shall attempt briefly to exemplify both kinds of inspirations or illuminations of the Holy Spirit in some few instances.

The Holy Spirit is said to fall or to be poured out upon the disciples five times only. The first instance of this miraculous effusion of the Holy Spirit was upon the apostles and their company. Acts 11:1-4, "And when the day of Pentecost was fully come, they were all with one accord in one place: and suddenly there came a sound, as of a rushing mighty wind; and it filled all the house where they were sitting; and there appeared unto them cloven tongues like as of fire; and sat upon each of them: and they were all filled with the holy ghost, and began to speak with other tongues, as the spirit gave them utterance." This company, upon whom the Holy Spirit miraculously descended, were about a hundred and twenty men and women, as appears from chapter 1:14-15 who are here said to be all with one accord in one place when the spirit fell upon them.

The second instance of this kind was a new (and probably similar) effusion of the Spirit upon the same apostles and company in answer to their prayer for boldness and courage when they were brought before the council. Acts 4:31, "And when they had prayed, the place was shaken where they were assembled together; and they were all filled with the holy ghost; and they spoke the word of God with boldness."

The third instance was when Saul was filled with the Holy Spirit (Acts 9:17 compared with 13:9).

A fourth instance was Cornelius and his household, who had the Holy Spirit poured out on them (Acts 10:45) as on the apostles and company at the beginning (Acts 11:15).

The fifth and last instance of the effusion of the Holy Spirit, without the laying on of hands, was on the first harvest of idolatrous Gentiles that were converted to the Christian faith, which was at Antioch in Pisidia (Acts 13:14-16, 42).

We are next to consider how the gifts of the Holy Spirit were received in a more mediate way, by the laying on of the apostles' hands. These miraculous gifts of the spirit were conferred upon many, and probably upon all true believers, wherever the apostles came. This will appear from these considerations:

Our blessed Savior promised this success to the apostles' ministry, that these signs shall follow them that believe: "in my name shall they cast out devils, they shall speak with new tongues, they shall take up serpents; and if they drink any deadly thing, it shall not hurt them, they shall lay hands on the sick, and they shall recover," (Mark 16:17-18). And the apostle Peter promises the three thousand in Acts 2:38 that upon their repentance and baptism, they should receive the gift of the Holy Spirit. And he likewise speaks of the Holy Spirit as given to them (i.e., to all) that obey him (Acts 5:32). The Holy Spirit is here spoken of as a witness to the resurrection and exaltation of Christ, whereof these gifts were unquestionable evidence (see Acts 2:33).

As soon as the Samaritans were converted by Philip, the apostles send Peter and John to them, that they might receive these gifts of the spirit, "and they laid their hands on them, and they received the Holy Ghost," (Acts 8:14-17). When Paul came to Ephesus and found certain disciples there, he asked them, "have ye received the Holy Ghost?" And finding they had not, he laid his hands on them; and the Holy Spirit came upon them, and they spoke with tongues and prophesied (Acts 19:1-6).

All the members of the church of Corinth seemed to have had these gifts in a very plentiful manner. They spoke with tongues, they prophesied, they interpreted. Every one of them had a psalm, a doctrine, a tongue, a revelation, an interpretation (verse 26). And that these gifts were not peculiar to the Corinthians, but were at least frequent in other churches also, appears from 1 Cor. 1:7, where the apostle tells them that they came behind in no gift. This plainly shows us that these gifts were in the other churches also, though not in a superior degree. The same thing appears from most of the other epistles to the churches, as may be seen from Gal. 3:2, 5, Eph. 1:13, 17, 1 Thess. 1:5, 20, 2 Tim. 1:6, 14, Heb. 6:4-5, 1 Pet. 1:12, and 1 John 2:20, among others.

These gifts of the Spirit were sudden illuminations of the mind by which the recipients were instantaneously imbued with the knowledge of a vast variety of languages (Acts 2, Acts 10:46), with an extensive knowledge of all needed doctrines of religion, whereby they were able to teach the mind of God clearly and powerfully (Rom. 2:10-12, 1 Peter 1:11-12), with the gift of prophecy, whereby they could foretell future events (Acts 11:28, 20:23), discern the spirits of others and tell the secrets of their hearts (1 Cor. 14:24, 25, 32), and judge of the fitness of persons for peculiar service in the church (Acts 13:1-2, 1 Tim. 1:18). They were frequently inspired with new revelations (1 Cor. 14:30), with the gift of interpreting as well as speaking foreign languages (1 Cor. 14:27), and with courage and fluency of speech on all occasions (1 Cor. 1:5). In addition, some of these had gifts of working miracles and of healing diseases, as appears from 1 Cor. 12:29-30. And all the apostles were instrumental by laying on of their hands to impart these gifts to others, wherever they themselves came. A summary of these several gifts may be found in 1 Cor. 12:8-10, "For to one is given by the spirit, the word of wisdom; to another, the word of knowledge by the same spirit; to another, faith by the same spirit; to another, the gifts of healing by the same spirit; to another, the working of miracles; to another, prophecy; to another, discerning of spirits; to another, divers kinds of tongues; to another, the interpretation of tongues."

Though these gifts of the Holy Spirit are sometimes in Scripture distinguished from miracles (particularly in Heb. 2:4), yet they are elsewhere expressly so denoted (see Gal. 3:5, 1 Cor. 12:29). They were at least certainly in their own nature miracles of the highest kind, such as could not have been done by the united power and skill of created spirits. For though we do not know what power angels have, we certainly know that it is the singular prerogative of the Father of spirits to enlarge the faculties of the soul of man in order to communicate those degrees of knowledge in an instant, which the keenest mind could not contain in an ordinary way without spending his whole life in full application to such studies. No man living can conceive how so much knowledge of so many arts and divine sciences could at once be imparted to anyone apart from him who is the author of our souls and who can enlarge our faculties as he pleases.

Let's consider more closely two of these gifts, which seem to have been common to most of the early believers: the gift of tongues and of prophecy. Would it have been possible for unlearned men and women to instantaneously possess such a vast variety of languages, in such perfection as to be able to use them with readiness and propriety, upon all proper occasions, without having their minds enlarged and this knowledge communicated to them by an infinite agent? Was it possible that any but God who alone foreknows all future events, could inspire these disciples with a spirit of prophecy, whereby they could foretell things to come? Or that any but he who knows the mind of the spirit could enable these men and women to discern the spirits and know the secret thoughts of other men's hearts? No surely! We may as well attribute all the perfections of God to a created being as these miraculous gifts and operations.

We have now considered some of those miracles performed by the power and authority of our blessed Lord both during his earthly ministry and after his resurrection, which are an evident attestation from heaven, not only to his divine mission and commission, but to the whole Christian institution. But it is time I proceed to the consideration of some further evidences that there were such miracles performed by our Lord Jesus Christ.

2. The reporters of these miracles have all the marks of honesty, integrity, and honor.

The doctrines they taught show the innocence and divine excellencies of their faith. The struggles they endured to propagate these doctrines show them to be sincere and in earnest in their profession. Further, they themselves both believed and practiced what they taught to others.

That they demonstrated excellence in their sanctity, as well as other extraordinary endowments, appears from their success. What irresistible charm so suddenly conquered the mighty opposition and constant obstacles in the hearts and lives of men against the gospel? How did so many people, cities, and countries convert from the opinions and manners which they had embraced from their infancy to those not only different, but contrary? The despised doctrine of the cross had no such charms in it, in the eye of carnal reason, to produce such wonderful effects. The base fishermen, by whom this amazing change was brought about had no advantage of military power, or of learned art and eloquence, to force those who heard them to submission. These evidences loudly proclaim the innocence and sanctity of their lives, without which they could not have been so regarded. These things clearly evidence that the apostles and other disciples possessed miraculous gifts; and did confirm their doctrine by miraculous operations, without which the seal of heaven would have been impossible to have persuaded so many to forsake their lusts and pleasures, their comfort, ease, and safety, for a persecuted religion and a crucified Savior.

In this way, we see that the witnesses were above reproach. And if we always allow for truth, confirmed by a number of faithful witnesses, we may surely rely on the joint testimony of such a number who could all truly appeal to the world that they had renounced the hidden things of dishonesty, not walking in craftiness nor handling the word of God deceitfully, but by manifestation of the truth had commended themselves to every man's conscience in the sight of God (2 Cor. 4:2).

3. These miraculous works and spiritual gifts reported by the sacred writers were matters of fact, in which it was impossible that they themselves could be deceived.

Our Lord's miracles were not matters of speculation or science, wherein the understandings of the disciples might be imposed upon, but matters of fact that came under the immediate recognition of their senses, such as they could see, hear, and feel and be ascertained of, by all possible means of certainty. These were not dark and obscure performances; they were not done in a corner, but most visibly, in the open light and in view of the world so there could be no possible opportunity of deceit.

These included multitudes of unquestionable miracles repeated again and again, in view of the same people who waited daily on their master and saw his wonderful works. These were not acts done before some few ignorant persons but in the face of the world, before multitudes of all sorts (beside the twelve apostles, seventy disciples, and many others that followed our Lord) who all acknowledged the facts, though they were not all converted by them.

To sum up all, these same witnesses assure us that they and many others beside them had themselves the miraculous gifts of the Holy Ghost and were employed in working the same or like miracles in Christ's name, and by his power and authority.

And now, will it not out-do the utmost strength of the imagination to find out how these witnesses could be deceived? Is it possible for any man to be more certain that he ever saw the sun, than these could be that they saw the sick healed, the dead raised, their Lord dying upon the cross, restored again to life, eating, drinking, and conversing familiarly with them forty days together, and ascending up to heaven before their eyes? Is it possible to have greater assurance of anything we do, or can do, than these could have, that they themselves, and multitudes beside them, had the gifts of languages, prophecy, and other miraculous powers and performed many miracles in the name of Christ?

The apostles rightly refered to these means of knowledge as "sure evidences" that they could not be deceived in the doctrines they taught. As 2 Peter 2:16 states, "For we have not followed cunningly devised fables, when we made known unto you the power and coming of our Lord Jesus Christ: but were eye-witnesses of his majesty." And 1 John 1:1, "That which we have heard, which we have seen with our eyes, which we have looked upon; and our hands have handled of the word of life."

4. As these witnesses were incapable of being deceived themselves in the facts reported by them, so were they without any possible temptation to deceive others by dispersing lies of this kind upon the world.

They had no motive or need to impose untruths on mankind regarding this matter. They could not make their case before princes and the great men of the world by a religion which they all opposed and persecuted. They had nothing to expect from their doctrine of the cross but to be (like their master) despised and rejected of men. This indeed was what their Lord foretold them and what they therefore expected when they undertook his service.

And now let us see whether riches and wealth could be their incentive, to publish such miracles and preach a crucified Savior. And nothing could be further from the reality they experienced. Poverty and penury and the want of all things were the necessary consequences of their extremely difficult and perilous travels through the world preaching this doctrine.

Or could a view to worldly ease and pleasure persuade them to this undertaking? Did they not know beforehand, as well as discover by experience, that they should be hated by all men for Christ's sake and that in every city bonds and afflictions would find them?

Upon the whole then, where can we find men in love with misery and ruin? Where can we see men court poverty and desire contempt, fetters, and bonds, and prefer both a miserable life and death to riches and honor, liberty, and ease? How then can we imagine that the apostles had some unforeseen motive to impose lies upon us in the case before us.

But what sets this matter in the clearest light is the fact that they sealed this testimony with their blood. Though men may be martyrs for a false religion, it must be only when they believe the religion which they die for is true. But there were multitudes who parted with their lives in confirmation of the Christian religion, that were themselves the coiners and forgers of the doctrine, if it was a lie. They could not themselves be deceived (as I have already proved) and therefore their report must necessarily be true, or else they must be charged with sacrificing their lives to confirm a lie of their own invention. That would be insanity indeed. To choose to suffer severe torments, the likes of which could never cause any one of them to retract or repent, to choose to dispose of all temporal comfort, with all worldly satisfactions, and even with life itself, which is to say they chose to destroy both body and soul forever, without any manner of reason or motive would indeed be insanity.

In this way, we have seen the strongest evidence of these truths, truths that any facts in the world were ever capable of. And we have stripped infidelity of all its armor and found just satisfaction that the apostles and other messengers of the gospel proved themselves to be ministers of God in their patience, afflictions, necessities, distresses, stripes, imprisonments, labors, watchings, and fastings (2 Cor. 6:4-5).

5. The reported miracles were matters of fact, in which it was impossible that these historians could deceive the world at the time when their narratives were published.

Let us first consider this case, with respect to the miracles performed by our Lord during his earthly ministry. These (as we noted before) were done publicly and openly, in the eye of the world, before some of the worst enemies of Christ, who regardless of all their vigilance and subterfuge could not detect any deceit or imposture. Nor did they charge the sacred narrative with falsehood or forgery. The narratives were written where these miracles were done, immediately after the performance of those wonderful transactions when they were fresh in everyone's memory, and when nobody could be ignorant of their truth or falsehood. Had any of these histories been false, it would certainly have been made known among those whom these miracles were both acted and published.

But what strengthens this argument is not only Christ's adversaries' assent to these matters of fact but their explicit attestation to some of them. For example, Josephus, the Jewish historian, gives us an epitome of the life, death, and resurrection of our Savior, whom he acknowledges a worker of great miracles. Tacitus, the Roman historian, informs us also of the time and circumstances of his death. I shall pass over many other remarks of this kind and only observe that the Jews universally from that time till now have acknowledged the truth of these miraculous operations, and informed us of many of them, whereof there is no mention in the gospels. They indeed sufficiently manifest their spite and malice against Christ by ascribing his miraculous works to wicked and unlawful arts; but the facts themselves they have never denied.

And now let us take a short view of the case, with respect to those miraculous gifts of the Holy Spirit, of which we have before treated. These, at the first effusion of the spirit, are said to have been openly manifested in view of devout men out of every nation under heaven, in a most public time, place, and manner. The whole world, therefore, had the advantage of discovering any fraud and of contradicting the story, if this narrative had been false. Besides, the apostle in almost all his epistles to the churches not only mentions these gifts, as what they themselves had experienced and were vested with, but frequently directs and exhorts them to a right use and improvement of them. This implies an appeal to the churches, that there were such gifts exercised among them.

And what adds strength to the evidence is that the apostle reproves both the Romans and Corinthians for their pride and conceit about these gifts, which occasionally resulted in contentions and divisions among them (Rom. 12:3-8, 1 Cor. 12-14). Now can it be imagined that any man in an epistle to a group of people among whom there are contentions would so particularly have directed them to the use, and so largely have reproved them for the abuse of such gifts if no such situation existed in any of them? And to further strengthen this evidence, the apostle puts the truth of his doctrine and his apostolical authority on this proof, when some of the churches were drawn away from his gospel and preferred the Jewish false apostles with their erroneous doctrines before him.

This was evidently the case of the Corinthians and Galatians, and especially the Corinthians, for the apostle urges this argument again and again in his first epistle to them, showing them that if he was not an apostle to others, yet without a doubt he was to them, for he says, "the seal of mine apostleship are ye in the Lord," (1 Cor. 9:2). What this seal or evidence of his apostleship was appears from his second epistle, where he resumes the same argument, particularly in 2 Cor. 12:12-13, "Truly the signs of an apostle were wrought among you, in signs and wonders and mighty deeds: for what is it wherein ye were inferior to other churches?" Here he rests the truth of his character and his gospel upon this single evidence (Gal. 3:1, 2, 5), "O foolish Galatians, who hath bewitched you, that ye should not obey the truth, *etc.* This only would I learn of you, received you the spirit by the works of the law; or by the hearing of faith? He therefore that ministers to you the spirit, and worketh miracles among you, does he do it by the works of the law, or by the hearing of faith?"

Can it be imagined that the apostle would put the proof of the truth of his Gospel, as well as his apostolical character, upon gifts of the Holy Spirit, conferred upon them by him, and that in a dispute with false apostles rivalling him in those churches, when there were no such gifts among them? Such a supposition is the height of absurdity. It was utterly impossible that these churches could be imposed on in this matter. And it was also impossible to impose upon the world around them who had every advantage and every opportunity to examine these facts to discover their truth or falsehood.

In summary, it is as clear as day that the world was not, nor could not have been fooled by these reports when they were first published. Also, the apostle boldly makes that appeal to King Agrippa in Acts 26:26, "For the king knows of these things, before whom also I speak freely: for I am persuaded, that none of these things are hidden from him: for this thing was not done in a corner."

6. We also have good assurance, that these narratives are handed down uncorrupted unto the present time.

The actions recorded by the sacred writers were notably famous in the world, as they incited great revolutions and even turned the world upside down by the conversion of so many from superstition and idolatry to the true worship of God. For these reasons, the records have been kept publicly in all ages and publicly preached by the ministers of Christ. This fact has given the most negligent enemy all advantage to discover and detect any fraudulent recording, had there been any such thing.

Besides, the doctrine taught in this blessed book rendered the professors of Christianity incapable of corrupting it, for no less than eternal damnation is pronounced against him that adds to or diminishes from one jot or tittle of the sacred canon. Should an angel from heaven teach any other doctrine than what is there taught, he is pronounced accursed. What temptation then could any have to alter these records, who kept them as their rule of life and charter for future glory?

They that were friends to Christianity and believed the history of these miracles could not corrupt them on purpose to procure damnation to their own souls. They that were enemies to Christianity and disbelieved these truths, would not corrupt them on purpose to prepare armor against their own infidelity.

But had any man attempted such a thing, it must have been without success. For these records were immediately in the hands of multitudes of people, translated into various languages and dispersed through all nations, making it impossible for the world to be deceived by such fraud and villainy. It would have been easier for a designing knave to corrupt our *Magna Carta*, frame a new body of laws for England, trump them upon us, and cause us to believe that these are and always have been the statutes of the nation than to imagine a similar corruption in these statutes of heaven. For the *Magna Carta* is in the hands of one nation only, but the New Testament (as I observed) is dispersed through the world and found in every copy of it to agree, in attesting these miraculous facts.

Thus, we have utmost certainty that the accounts of these facts, now in our hands, are the uncorrupted writings of the apostles and evangelists. And thus, do we see the promise fulfilled, "that the word of the Lord shall endure forever, even that word which by the gospel is preached unto us," (1 Peter 1:25).

We are now prepared to consider,

III. That these miracles, which I have proved to have been performed by our Lord Jesus Christ, both before and after his passion, give full evidence that he was approved of God and had his mission from him.

This may be evidenced by the following considerations.

1. These miracles are certainly the work of God himself, as his direct agency is plainly visible in them.

If it is possible for any created beings to work a true miracle, even still their agency must be always under God's control. Otherwise, the infernal powers might interrupt the revolutions of nature and bring the world into a chaos. Such miracles, therefore, whoever the instrumental agent may be, must acknowledge the works of God, as God is himself as near to the effect when he uses instruments as when he acts immediately without them.

If the facts are true, (as I've already proved them to be), all the world must own that the wonderful works which our Lord Jesus Christ performed while on earth were the mighty works of God; that those sacred gifts which we have considered were certainly divine. It was therefore a just and natural inference that Nicodemus made in John 3:2, "Rabbi, we know that thou art a teacher come from God: for no man can do these miracles that thou do, except God be with him."

2. It is contrary to the goodness and faithfulness of God to justify an impostor or confirm a falsehood by miracles.

It is impossible in this imperfect state for us to have better evidence that any person or doctrine is from God than these miracles. By these we have visibly before our eyes God's own immediate agency. We see the extraordinary display of his omnipotent power; we certainly know that there is the immediate finger of God in these mighty works. And our Lord Jesus produces this seal of heaven as a voucher to his doctrine and authority. He declares himself to be the expected Messiah, and these surprising wonders are done to confirm it. He publishes by his disciples his resurrection from the dead, and his ascension into heaven, which are also confirmed by the same evidence. Both he and his disciples appeal to the senses of mankind that he is indeed who he declares himself to be, the son of God and Lord of life and glory; and he has indeed been declared the son of God with power by his resurrection from the dead. God justifies the appeal from heaven and gives the visible testimony of miracles, both before and after his crucifixion, that he is his beloved son in whom he is well pleased.

Infidelity can therefore have no place of retreat. We must believe in this Savior or disbelieve the attestation of the God of truth. If we are deceived, the deceit is inevitable; and the best men in the world who have the sincerest love for God and despise whatever is desirable or terrible, for his sake and service, are deluded in their most important concerns by God himself. Now can it be imagined, can we entertain the least thought, that infinite holiness would thus justify a fraudulent imposture; that infinite truth and faithfulness would affirm his seal to a lie; and that infinite wisdom and goodness would thus give up the world to unavoidable error and delusion? No surely! To refuse this testimony is not only stupidity and madness, but obstinacy and malice, not far removed from the nature of devils.

Thus, we see two most faithful witnesses – the power and veracity of God – verifying the truth of our Savior's heavenly mission. For this reason, we must either divest ourselves of reason and humanity or yield to the irresistible force of our Lord's argument posed in John 10:37-38, "If I do not the works of my Father, believe me not: but if I do, though ye believe not me, believe the works, that ye may know and believe, that the Father is in me, and I in him."

Before I proceed to a particular application of this doctrine, I would here more particularly observe that whatever has been said to verify the divine mission of our Lord Jesus Christ, may equally serve to confirm the truth and heavenly origin of the whole Christian religion. The doctrine, and the person of Christ, are authorized of God, by the same seal of heaven. If the Lord

Jesus is indeed the son of God and redeemer of mankind, his institutions must be worthy of his glorious nature and office. If the apostles, and other holy writers, were indeed commissioned and inspired of him, they were equally incapable to deceive us in an affair of everlasting consequence.

If we are demanded to answer how we can be certain that the sacred penmen were divinely inspired in writing the New Testament, I would respond by saying we have the same assurance of this as we have of the matters of fact reported by them. They themselves attest it. They have proved themselves persons of integrity. They could not be deceived in this matter but must certainly know whether they were acted on by a heavenly inspiration or not. They could have no temporal inducement to promote false doctrine upon us when they sealed both with their blood. And we have the same security, that both have been handed down uncorrupted to our times.

Further, God declared from heaven his approval of their doctrine by the gifts of the Holy Spirit conferred upon them. Christ promised them this seal to their commission, that the works that he did, they should do also; and greater works than these, when he was gone to the Father (John 14:12). And that he would send the promise of his Father upon them, and endue them with power from on high (Luke 24:49). This promise was visibly verified to them. The Holy Spirit did (as was promised) descend from heaven upon them and instantly invested them with the knowledge of various languages (so that they could speak them with their peculiar idioms and accents) and with the several other gifts which we have before considered, and by which they were qualified to travel throughout the nations and universally publish the glad tidings of salvation. Everywhere they went their doctrine was confirmed by leaving behind them some miraculous blessing, either upon the body, the mind, or both. Serpents were tamed, devils ejected, the sick healed, and the dead raised at their word. And we have the most unquestionable evidence of these facts that we can have of anything not done in our own sight, as you heard before. We are therefore constrained to give a full and entire assent to all the doctrines of Christianity, as what God has born witness to, both with signs and wonders and diverse miracles and gifts of the Holy Spirit, according to his own will (Heb. 2:4).

Conclusion.

This doctrine teaches us what indispensable obligations we live under, to bring forth a life of holy obedience to this precious Savior whom the Father has sanctified, sent into the world, and thus incontestably declared to be his beloved Son in whom he is well pleased.

I hope that what you have heard has brought you without any hesitancy to conclude with Philip in John 1:45, "We have found him, of whom Moses in the law and the prophets did write, Jesus of Nazareth the son of Joseph." In this way, I also hope you'll all be ready to address our Lord as in the words of Nathanael, "Rabbi, thou art the son of God, thou art the King of Israel."

But it concerns you also to consider that Christ came to save his people from their sins. He came to redeem us from all iniquity and to purify unto himself a peculiar people, zealous of good works. And the design of the gospel is to turn men from darkness unto light and from the power of Satan unto God. Christianity consists not merely in speculation, but in practice. We must not only give our assent to the truth of the gospel, but give up our hearts to Christ. The faith which he requires is not a slight superficial belief that he is the Redeemer of mankind, but such a faith as will form us into subjection and obedience to himself.

If we believe that Jesus Christ is our only Savior, then what stupidity, what madness is it, to reject or neglect him and his tendered salvation, to embrace our lusts and perish in them! If we believe the truth of the gospel, can we be deaf to all its gracious invitations and despise all its promises and threatenings as if they were mere fables! Are we lifted up to heaven by the exhibitions of so great a salvation; and shall we nevertheless cast ourselves down to hell by willfully refusing it and preferring our sinful pleasures before it!

This is not only to reproach our holy profession, but to bring such a degree of guilt upon our own souls, as will render us most inexcusable and most aggravatedly miserable at last. Therefore, let those that name the name of Christ depart from iniquity. Let his throne be set up in our hearts, that all our faculties may bow down to him. Let us choose him for our portion, seek an interest in him with unrelenting earnestness and diligence, depend upon him as the Lord our righteousness, and live to him with our whole hearts. If we thus come to him, he will in no wise cast us out; otherwise, our most flourishing profession will not secure us from having our portion with hypocrites and unbelievers in the day of retribution.

 And yet I know that some may be ready to say, how shall we know in what way to serve Christ to his acceptance? There are so many different sects and parties among professed Christians, each of whom censure and condemn the other, that we do not know where to find rest for the soles of our feet; nor in which of these different paths to steer our course for heaven.

 This objection, I confess, may produce trouble and difficulty for some sincere and well-minded persons, as well as offence and scandal to those of a wavering and unsettled faith. I shall therefore spend the remaining time before us in clarifying this difficulty and in giving you plain directions, how you may be infallibly sure of serving Christ acceptably here, and of inheriting the reward of a patient continuance in well-doing hereafter.

 1. Labor to make sure of a true and lively faith in Jesus Christ.

No one will see heaven who does not possess a true unfeigned faith; nor will any true believer ever fall short of eternal life. Faith transforms the soul into the divine nature; and God cannot be displeased with his own image, wherever it is. Our great concern therefore is, to fly to the blood of Christ for cleansing and to his righteousness for justification; to lie at the footstool of his grace with a humble sense of our own nothingness, and with continual pursuit of the sanctifying influences of his Holy Spirit by which we may receive Christ Jesus the Lord and walk in him. If we are chargeable with many mistakes in matters not essential to salvation, yet clothed with the righteousness of Christ, we shall appear without spot and blameless, the sons of God, without rebuke, in the great day of trial. In that day it will not be asked, who is of Paul? Who of Apollos? Or who of Cephas? But who is savingly united unto Jesus Christ? And then shall the promise be certainly verified that is found in John 3:16, that "whosoever believeth in him, shall not perish, but have everlasting life."

2. Evidence the truth and sincerity of your faith by a holy and heavenly life.

Faith without holiness is as a carcass without breath. Whoever is born of God does not (cannot) commit sin (1 John 3:9). The allowed practice of any sin, either of omission or commission, is inconsistent with the quality and grace of a regenerate state. There is no middle ground between a saint and an unbeliever; so, to entertain hopes of our justification while living an idle or sensual life is to compass ourselves about with sparks of our own kindling that will expose us at last to lie down in sorrow.

The best means to discover the sincerity of our profession and the safety of our state is to show our faith by our works. If we are true believers, our hearts are purified by faith. And if we are pure in heart, we shall see God. Let us then walk as becomes the gospel of Christ. Let us cleanse ourselves from all filthiness of flesh and spirit and live in perfect holiness and in the fear of God. And God will prove himself to be no respecter of persons, but in every nation, and in every sect and every party, he that fears God and works righteousness shall be accepted of him (Acts 19:34-35).

3. Embrace and live by those doctrines which tend most to debase yourselves and magnify the free grace of God.

The whole of our salvation, from the first corner stone to its complete perfection in glory, is a continual series of infinite free grace. "By grace are we saved through faith, and that not of ourselves, it is the gift of God," (Eph. 2:8). Mercy must shine forth in its brightest glory if such guilty rebels as we are saved, and such brands are plucked out of the fire of sin and hell.

If we ever hope to find acceptance with our Lord Jesus Christ, we must come to him with a spiritual understanding that we are poor, and miserable, and wretched, and blind, and naked, that we deserve nothing but wrath and can do nothing that will entitle us to his favor. We must come to him both for power to serve him and for a gracious acceptance of our services for his own sake, and not for ours. We must remember that we are indigent beggars that live only upon alms; that we are criminal delinquents that are kept from execution by mere divine goodness and therefore, have our whole dependence in Christ, to do all in us and for us; to be to us wisdom, righteousness, sanctification, and redemption. In a word, we must not depend upon works of righteousness that we have done or can do; but count all as loss and dung that we may win Christ and be found in him, not having our own righteousness, which is of the law, but that which is through the faith of Christ, the righteousness which is of God by faith (Phil. 3:8-9).

It is remarkable that most of the heresies that have ever sprung up in the church have some way or other exposed those fundamental articles of our faith and hope, the sovereignty of free grace in our sanctification, and the necessity of Christ's imputed righteousness to our justification and acceptance with God. So, do not unite with that assembly who depreciates the grace of God and the satisfaction of Christ, and thus subverts the whole scope and design of the gospel. Let us avoid all such errors, and rather venture our salvation only upon unmerited mercy, hoping to be justified freely by God's grace through the redemption that is in Jesus Christ (Rom. 3:24). Let Christ have all the glory of our salvation now, that we may hereafter join with those that shall ascribe glory and dominion, for ever and ever, to him that loved us and washed us from our sins in his own blood, and made us kings and priests unto God and his Father.

4. Religiously attend all the ordinances and institutions of Christ.

Let the word of Christ be your rule of worship, your directory in the service of God. Let it be your care to keep the ordinances as they have been delivered to you in the holy scriptures. It must be the character of every true Christian that he endeavors to walk in all the commandments and ordinances of the Lord, blameless (Luke 1:6). Though the means of grace may lack all that external pomp, beauty, or ornament that captures a carnal eye, they are the institutions of God which he therefore owns and blesses. It has pleased God by the foolishness of his ordinances to save them that believe (1 Cor. 1:21). And we have no reason to hope for salvation in the contempt or willful neglect of them. If we would find Christ, we must seek him where he walks, in the midst of his golden candlesticks. If we would inherit the blessing, we must watch daily at Christ's gates and wait at the posts of his doors. Whoever pretends any other way to heaven than this path of ordinances which God has marked out for us, after the first and second admonition reject them.

5. Concern yourselves as little as possible with matters of doubtful dispute. But where you must be of one party or another, choose the charitable side.

There will be different sentiments among Christians as long as we are on this side of heaven. We shall not come to an exact unity in all articles of faith until that which is in part shall be done away; and we know even as also we are known. But cannot we bear with the different thoughts, as well as different complexions of those that agree with us in the essentials of Christianity; and receive one another, as Christ also received us, to the glory of God?

It is true that we cannot ourselves be of two contrary persuasions. But how shall weak Christians act in this case? How shall they know which party to join? It is impossible that I should now descend to particular directions in this case; I must therefore content myself with commending that general rule of the apostle in 2 Tim. 2:22, "Follow righteousness, faith, charity, peace, with them that call on the Lord out of a pure heart." Never join yourselves with those that are for cutting off all the protestant churches but themselves from the fold of Christ, nor expect to be saved by damning everybody but yourselves.

Finally, constantly and fervently commit your souls to the keeping and conduct of our Lord Jesus Christ.

We are liable to a thousand mistakes; but we have a safe and sure pilot upon whom we may boldly depend. If we commit our way to him, he will bring it to pass. If he leaves us to lesser mistakes, he will save us from damning errors, unless our own sin and spiritual laziness put us outside of his protection. We must therefore not only carefully and diligently judge ourselves; but with greatest earnestness and constancy seek the directions of his Holy Spirit, and wrestle with him by earnest prayer that he will search us and try us and see if there be any wicked way in us and lead us in the way everlasting; that he will guide us by his counsel, and afterward bring us to glory. And in that way, we may with courage conclude with the apostle in 2 Tim. 1:12, "I know whom I have trusted; and am persuaded, that he is able to keep that which I have committed to him against that day."

FINIS

Other New and Helpful Works from Puritan Publications

5 Marks of Christian Resolve
by C. Matthew McMahon

A Biblical Guide to Hearing and Studying the Word
by Richard Greenham, et. al.

A Watchman Over Christ's Church
by C. Matthew McMahon

Attending the Lord's Table
by Henry Tozer (1602-1650)

Discovering the Glorious Love of Christ
by John Durant (1620-1686)

God is Our Refuge and Our Strength
by George Gipps (n.d.)

God, a Rich Supply of All Good
by Nathaniel Holmes (1599–1678)

I Am for You: God's Power in Supporting His People
by C. Matthew McMahon

Reformation of the Heart, Soul and Mind
by C. Matthew McMahon

Remembering Your Creator
by Matthew Mead (Meade) (1630-1699)

Other Works

Repentance and Prayer
by Ralph Brownrig (1592–1659)

The Blessed God
by Daniel Burgess (1645-1713)

The Cursed Family, or the Evil of Neglecting Family Prayer by
Thomas Risley (1630–1716)

The Excellent Name of God
by Jeremiah Burroughs (1599-1646)

The Five Principles of the Gospel
by C. Matthew McMahon

The Great Mystery of God's Providence, and Other Works by
George Gifford (1547-1620)

The Kingdom of Heaven is Upon You
by C. Matthew McMahon

The Sweetness of Divine Meditation
by William Bridge (1600-1670)

The Wonders of Jesus
by Jeremiah Burroughs (1599-1646)

A Devotional on Our Savior's Death and Passion
by Charles Herle (1598-1659)

www.ingramcontent.com/pod-product-compliance
Lightning Source LLC
Chambersburg PA
CBHW020205090426
42734CB00008B/944